20⁰⁰

100 Silent Films

100 SILENT FILMS

BFI Screen Guides

Bryony Dixon

A BFI book published by Palgrave Macmillan

First published in 2011 by
PALGRAVE MACMILLAN

on behalf of the

BRITISH FILM INSTITUTE
21 Stephen Street, London W1T 1LN
www.bfi.org.uk

There's more to discover about film and television through the BFI. Our world-renowned archive, cinemas, festivals, films, publications and learning resources are here to inspire you.

Palgrave Macmillan in the UK is an imprint of Macmillan Publishers Limited, registered in England, company number 785998, of Houndmills, Basingstoke, Hampshire RG21 6XS. Palgrave Macmillan in the US is a division of St Martin's Press LLC, 175 Fifth Avenue, New York, NY 10010. Palgrave Macmillan is the global academic imprint of the above companies and has companies and representatives throughout the world. Palgrave® and Macmillan® are registered trademarks in the United States, the United Kingdom, Europe and other countries.

Series cover design: Paul Wright
Cover image: *Metropolis* (Fritz Lang, 1927), Ufa
Series design: Ketchup/couch
Set by Cambrian Typesetters, Camberley, Surrey
Printed in China

This book is printed on paper suitable for recycling and made from fully managed and sustained forest sources. Logging, pulping and manufacturing processes are expected to conform to the environmental regulations of the country of origin.

British Library Cataloguing-in-Publication Data
A catalogue record for this book is available from the British Library
A catalog record for this book is available from the Library of Congress
10 9 8 7 6 5 4 3 2 1
20 19 18 17 16 15 14 13 12 11

ISBN 978–1–84457–308–0 (pbk)
ISBN 978–1–84457–309–7 (hbk)

Contents

Acknowledgments

I would like to thank Rebecca Barden, commissioning editor, and Sophia Contento of BFI/Palgrave Macmillan for their professionalism and patience, and my managers Heather Stewart, Robin Baker and Patrick Russell for allowing me time to research and write this Guide. I would also like to thank my colleagues in the curatorial unit of the BFI National Archive, many of whom helped out with advice and encouragement: in particular, Mark Duguid, Patrick Russell (again), Michael Brooke, Upekha Bandaranayake, Nathalie Morris, Nigel Arthur and Jez Stewart. I am also grateful for help and inspiration from the silent film fraternity – too many to name, but a special thankyou to Luke McKernan, Laraine and Sue Porter, Neil Brand, Paul Marygold, Phil Carli, Thomas Christensen, Camille Blot-Wellens, Lenny Borger, David Mayer and Stephen Horne – as well as the organisers and programmers of the Cinema Ritrovato in Bologna and the Giornate del Cinema Muto Pordenone festivals.

Personal thanks and apologies are due to my family and friends, who have had to put up with a deal of whingeing and inattention – the ex 'steps' posse (you know who you are), especially Mark, who got the worst of it, Sorrel, Garth, Jo and all the little Dixons.

Introduction

Silent film is an art form marooned by history. A wonderfully strange hybrid, it is arguably less close to modern 'cinema' as we know it, than to opera and television. The feature-length silent drama, as performed with its combination of images and musical accompaniment, is perhaps most analogous to opera, with its own vernacular and appeal to obsessives and enthusiasts. At its most grand, on the big screen with a full orchestral accompaniment, it is magnificent, permitting a depth of emotional engagement rarely found in other fields of cinema – a consequence of the concentration required to 'read' the drama.
The range of other types of film in the silent era – documentary, newsreel, interest films, travelogues, short comedies, animation and advertising – were exhibited in mixed programmes, so that an evening's entertainment at the fairground in the 1900s, or at one of the freshly built cinemas in the 1910s, would in some ways resemble the 'varied diet' of an evening's television. It is helpful to make this analogy, because silent film is often seen as cinema that is 'broken' or inadequate.

It should also be pointed out that unlike most of the categories of films in this series of guides, silent cinema is not a genre; it's the first thirty-five years of film history, a record starting over a hundred years ago of human endeavour, a complex negotiation between art and commerce, and a union of creativity and technology. It contains many of the genres we would recognise from later sound films (Westerns, thrillers, horror, romantic comedy, etc.) and some of its own.
Nearly every important aspect of film – its techniques, tricks and special effects, and its language – was established in the silent era. It marked the start of our fascination with the moving image as a disseminator of

information as well as mass entertainment, spawning the celebrity culture so dominant today.

This book aims to be a welcoming and inspiring introduction for the general reader who might be attracted to the subject, presenting a range of classic titles, together with more unexpected choices, to break down some common misconceptions. At the same time, it will try to place the films in their historical and cultural context. Thanks to the alphabetical format of these BFI Screen Guides, it is not director or auteur led; it avoids pigeonholing films as 'primitive' because they were made before the film-making grammar familiar to us today had had a chance to develop; nor does it isolate films in their national silos. The Guide goes directly to the heart of the matter of silent cinema – that is, the films themselves – with the object of encouraging the reader to seek out and engage with these works. The entries aim to reveal the characteristics and development of the silent film, the principal genres and movements, and to indicate continuities with later film. There are a few '-isms' attached to writing on silent film which it is as well to be aware of – major artistic or aesthetic movements of the time such as Impressionism, Expressionism and Surrealism; while for forms such as slapstick or melodrama, newsreel or trick films, some knowledge of history and the chronology of basic film technology is useful.

It is important to stress that this is not a 'best of' book. These are 100 films that tell you something interesting about silent cinema. It is perhaps, in the manner of Neil McGregor's *History of the World in 100 Objects*, a brief history of silent cinema in 100 films. It is not a beauty contest, nor is it intended to be exhaustively representative. The list aims to be thought-provoking and inspirational without ignoring the classics.

Just 100 titles for thirty-five years of film history necessarily means that this is a starting point and not the last word on the subject. The selection includes films made in any part of the world after 1895 and before the early 1930s (with the exception of one twenty-first-century silent). It encompasses fiction and non-fiction film and gives as much attention to film of a minute's duration as to a full-length feature. The list covers many types of films – animation, comedy, actuality, interest, travelogue, advertising, newsreel, drama and the experimental. As is common with studies of silent cinema, there is a bias towards the fiction feature film. This reflects the industry at its height, but also helps make the subject as accessible as possible for those interested in the wider world of cinema for whom the feature film might be a natural entry point. I have included films made by some of the great 'stars' of the time, because the star system that began in the silent age had such an impact on the development of the cinema. There is a slight bias towards British titles, which may raise an eyebrow or two, for which I make no apology: this is principally my field and this is a British book. I have omitted pornography on the grounds that it isn't generally available, not because it doesn't exist.

All the films in the list are extant, because it is primarily my ambition that the book will inspire readers to want to see some of the films for themselves. This is germane, because survival rates for silent film are so much lower than for later sound film – with the end of the silent era, a great many films, having no further commercial life, were destroyed, while time has done for many of the rest. The survivors are available to a greater or lesser extent – many are released commercially or are regularly programmed at cinematheques and film clubs. Some will only be accessible through film institutes and archives. It has not been realistic before now to expect a reasonable proportion of the films in such a guide to be available for the general public to view but the digital revolution is increasing this availability all the time.

I hope that the breadth of films in the selection will open up this thirty-five-year period in a way that dispels some of the very persistent myths that have grown up around it. It may be helpful at this point to say a word or two about basic developments to situate the films in their chronological context. First, on the issue of film length: in the beginning, film was short – only a minute or so of running time. Initially, film-makers were working in a world where short 'variety' items made up a main entertainment. In the very early days, films were exhibited as an act in touring fairground shows or as a 'turn' in music halls. Films in this volume such as *Panorama du Grand Canal vu d'un bateau**, *The Big Swallow** or the Mitchell & Kenyon film* would have been exhibited in this way. At first, the novelty of movement itself was attraction enough, but film-makers rapidly began to add other features to sustain their appeal. Even at this early stage, films were sometimes in colour or had soundtracks recorded on cylinder or disc. Dramatic reconstructions of topical events were another way of adding appeal. These were not 'fake' newsreels, as is often supposed, but dramatic sketches intended to illustrate events in the news in much the same way as artists sketches did in the papers. This kind of reconstruction was also firmly established in the music-hall tradition and there was no intention to suggest that these dramatisations were 'real'. Audiences of the 1890s and 1900s were neither primitive nor stupid, and there is no evidence to suggest that they mistook scenes clearly filmed in England for the South African veldt or China, or that they ran away in a panic from on-screen trains, or, for that matter, that they were any rowdier than audiences today.

As films got longer in the 1900s, they began to separate into distinct genres, but were still exhibited as a mixed programme in venues including shop fronts, church halls, theatres, music halls and, increasingly, purpose-built cinemas. Films confined to the 20-minute film programme prevalent in the music hall, taken out of its line-up with live acts, could expand according to their type. News items were often necessarily brief, interest films (such as travelogues, industrial films, science and nature, etc.) settled at about 10–12 minutes, comedies and dramas at a reel, which could last up to 20 minutes. We can imagine a typical evening's entertainment that includes a 'topical' like *The Derby 1913**, 'interest' films such as *Birth of a Flower** or *Glimpses at Bird Life**, a stencil colour drama like *Mariée du château maudit** or a fairy film such as *The Talisman**, plus a comedy like *Premier prix de violoncelle**.

By the teens, the more settled nature of the film business in the new cinema led to greater specialisation and the rise of the regular newsreels, one- and two-reel comedies, the sensationalist serials, and longer and longer dramas. It is at this point that the star system kicked in and

Hollywood began to emerge as an economic force. Industrial and commercial changes led to the development of special 'features' – long dramas from Denmark and Italy (and subsequently from everywhere else) – of over an hour in length. A resilient format, like the novel, the 90-minute feature began to dominate the cinema programmes, and is very much with us a century later. Short films, however, continued to be the bread and butter of production, while features prompted the industry to invest ever-larger sums in stars, talented directors and crew.

In the 1920s, film began to be studied. Film clubs and societies sprang up, and other types of artistic film emerged in this milieu, outside the commercial film world. Film language and grammar continued to develop in both artistic and commercial environments, as the industry became more integrated and production values climbed. Film-making advanced spectacularly, with all sorts of skills becoming specialised, including acting for the screen. It is another common myth that silent film acting is melodramatic and overly theatrical. Inevitably, cinema adopted the style of the theatre at first, but this soon changed. You will search in vain for a girl tied to railway tracks, except in comedies, which are spoofing melodramas of the stage not the screen. By this time, too, comedy had developed to a peak that is rarely surpassed even now.

It is impossible to appreciate silent film's power without recognising the contribution of the ever-present musical accompaniment. This might be a solo piano or a small band, depending on the space available and depth of the exhibitor's pockets, but by the end of the silent era, accompaniments could be very elaborate orchestral scores (even the occasional experimental work) specially composed and performed by an orchestra worthy of the finest theatres. It is the combination of music and image that makes silent film a different experience to sound cinema.

With a critical mass of restored material from the archives and sustainable specialist silent film programming at festivals and cinematheques, we are enjoying something of a golden age for silent film. The digital revolution in the last few years has fed the massive resurgence of interest in silent cinema with a steady flow of titles available on DVD or Blu-Ray, numerous online resources and a proliferation of courses teaching silent film. The huge upsurge in the popularity of family history, as well as film history, sparked off by the digitisation of historical records has led to broadcasters losing some of their fear of 'old' film, producing some valuable documentaries. Where once we might have waited years to see a specific film or travelled thousands of miles to consult a film trade journal, today we might find both brought to our computer screens. While refreshing my memory of the 4-hour *Nibelungen Saga* for this book, I was able to see the whole film in 7-minute segments on YouTube in surprisingly good quality and with a full orchestral score. All the same, there is still much for the archivists to uncover and for researchers and audiences to discover; after all, as an academic discipline, the study of film is relatively young.

I hope this guide will help those who might be tempted to join in this work, as well as interest those who are just curious, and I hope that it will provide some stimulating routes through this fascinating subject and reveal some of the range and diversity of these films, from the work of familiar artists like Hitchcock or Lang, whose roots were in silent film, to the magnificent scope of *Napoleon* or *Metropolis*, to the briefest flash of ingenuity like *The Big Swallow*. References to other entries in the book are marked with an asterisk to allow ease of cross-reference. There are, no doubt, several unforgivable omissions: interesting directors, important films and subgenres. If I have left out some of your favourites, sorry – I have left out some of mine too. And by the way, it will not be necessary to die after you have seen these 100 films.

The Adventures of Dollie
US, 1908 – 12 mins
D. W. Griffith

Billy Bitzer, who came to be D. W. Griffith's cameraman of choice, claims to have given Griffith some advice when he took up his directing job at the Biograph studio in 1908, outlining the five essential elements for a successful film – drama, danger, rescue, love and comedy. I doubt that Bitzer would find many people who would disagree with him back in 1908, or indeed now, for these are the essential elements in most conventional works of cinematic storytelling; moreover, it was probably unnecessary advice for the fledgling director, who had earlier that year starred in a film that utilised these elements to perfection. The actor – Laurence Griffith, as D. W. was known then – played the father of a kidnapped baby in the Edison drama *Rescued from an Eagle's Nest*. The film is set in a wild mountainous region, from where the baby is carried off by an eagle and must be rescued by the daring descent of a precipitous cliff, a fight with the wild bird and the retrieval of the child from the rocky ledge. It is well paced and structured, and the special effects showing the baby carried high above the earth in the eagle's talons are spectacular.

Griffith had only to learn from this film in his first directing job to guarantee a sure-fire hit, which is more less what happened. *The Adventures of Dollie* was another 'kidnapped child in peril' story: this time, three-year-old Dollie is playing with her parents down by the river when she is snatched by an aggrieved gypsy. The child is taken to the gypsy's caravan and hidden, gagged, in a barrel when the pursuing father comes to search the camp. Only inches away from the child, he fails to find her and the gypsies move on. As they cross the river, however, the barrel comes loose and falls off the caravan into the river, where it floats inexorably towards a weir. The barrel falls over the weir and continues on, fetching up by the same stretch of riverside where Dollie had been playing with her parents earlier, and near to where a boy is fishing. The boy retrieves the barrel, then jumps back in surprise when he hears a noise coming from inside. The father arrives and opens the barrel to discover his small daughter none the worse for her adventures.

There is nothing remarkable about the plot – it is faintly ludicrous, the gypsies are portrayed in an unsympathetic way that would no longer be tolerated today, and there are no close-ups (or none that survive in the existing print) to help the audience develop a particular connection with Dollie or any of the other characters. And yet, I have seen *The Adventures of Dollie* several times with modern audiences and they all respond similarly, with recognition. It makes people smile. The movie is a little proto-feature film – like a seed. Sprinkle it with a few subplots and swell to an hour's running time and it would make a perfect little American drama that generations of us are familiar with. The Edison film, nice as it is, doesn't have that effect. The miniscule differences that Griffith contributed included greater naturalism, which steered clear of obvious trick effects, and better acting. Most importantly, however, was the improved continuity – for example, notice how the gypsy just manages to stuff the child in the barrel and batten down the lid as the father comes running into view, or later, when the barrel drifts into shot as the boy is fishing in the river. Small differences perhaps, but they would have big consequences for the future of film.

Dir: D. W. Griffith; **Ph**: Arthur Marvin; **Cast**: Arthur V. Johnson, Gladys Egan, Linda Arvidson, Charles Inslee, Madeline West.

Alfred Butterworth & Sons, Leaving the Works, Glebe Mills, Hollinford
UK, 1901 – 1.5 mins
Mitchell & Kenyon

A relatively recent find in the UK of over 800 original camera negatives from the Edwardian era has revolutionised our understanding of a subgenre of films which you won't find in the general histories. Produced by the firm of Mitchell & Kenyon, these are now categorised as 'local films' and represent the company's response to the popularity of films distributed by the Lumière brothers and others in Britain from 1896 onwards. Where the Lumières, after their initial success at home, sent out cameramen such as Alexandre Promio to film cities all round the world, Mitchell & Kenyon focused primarily on their locality, the north of England, building on the strategy of *La Sortie des usines Lumière* (1895), which showed workers leaving the factory en masse, in order to capture both the interesting movement and the prospect it offered of getting as many people in the frame as possible.

The commercial angle seized on by Mitchell & Kenyon was to exploit the audience's natural curiosity about the new moving pictures and their desire, nurtured by clever publicity, to 'see yourselves as other see you'. Rather than waiting for films to filter through from the big cities, they would 'take them and make them' on the spot. The films proved an instant success with audiences and were shown by fairground showmen and local exhibitors all over the region. While workers leaving the factories remained a favourite, they were soon supplemented by local events of all kinds – sporting fixtures, ship embarkations, high days and holidays, calendar customs, local processions, 'phantom rides' filmed from trams or trains, and street scenes.

Alfred Butterworth & Sons, Leaving the Works, Glebe Mills, Hollinford was typical of the factory-gate film. Shot in August 1901, it was commissioned by local showmen to be screened at the Wakes week holiday. The workers pour out through the gates straight towards the camera – women in shawls, men in caps and shirtsleeves file past, along with a large number of children carrying lunch baskets for their parents or siblings. The children are encouraged by the showmen or film-makers to come up to the camera, which they do in profusion, some larking about, some just staring into the lens. It is a strange sensation for the modern viewer, particularly when seen on the big screen, to look directly into the eyes and connect with someone from a century ago who is long dead. Young boys, especially, demonstrate real curiosity about the camera and a wish to be seen. Contemporary viewers can't help speculating on the fate of these youthful individuals, many of whom would have been of an age to die in the trenches of World War I. These local films furnish us with an enormous amount of information about our forebears, their working lives and leisure pursuits, as well as a host of detail about people and place, with an immediacy that only film can convey.

Prod: Mitchell & Kenyon.

Alice in Wonderland
UK, 1903 – 8 mins (originally 12 mins)
Percy Stow

This film version of Lewis Carroll's classic children's book, *Alice's Adventures in Wonderland*, was produced in a pivotal year for the development of film. Longer films with developing narratives, whether in sequential tableaux (as with *Alice*) or logically linked scenes (such as *Daring Daylight Robbery*), had arrived. *Alice* barely survives, in an incomplete and deteriorated version at the BFI, but in its day it was a prestige production, expensive at £20 or a staggering £25 in colour. It is worth quoting the entry in the Hepworth catalogue for 1904:

> The interesting and beautiful story by Lewis Carroll of 'Alice's Adventures in Wonderland' is familiar to most people, and in producing a film of this well-known tale, the lines of the book have been strictly adhered to, and in nearly every instance Sir John Tenniel's famous illustrations have been reproduced in animated form with remarkable fidelity. The film is composed of sixteen scenes, dissolving very beautifully from one to another, but preceded, where necessary for the elucidation of the story, by short descriptive titles.

This accurately describes the film, which, at 800 feet, was the longest yet produced in Britain, and resembled more closely the magic-lantern entertainments of that era than narrative film as we understand it today. Each scene, though occurring in the correct order in relation to the book, was autonomous and based on the illustrations rather than the text. The selection was based largely on the practicality of filming such a scene – imagine trying to reproduce the caucus race or the trial scene, which are, in fact, along with the hookah-smoking caterpillar, the only significant omissions. Hepworth was not one for elaborate theatrical sets and proudly explained, again from the 1904 catalogue: 'No pantomime or stage effect is introduced in this film;

The first ever screen version of *Alice in Wonderland*, 1903

the whole of the various scenes having been produced in pretty natural surroundings.'

This was entirely deliberate. Hepworth had the use of some fine formal gardens at Mount Felix, a grand house not far from his Walton-on-Thames studios, and could take advantage of the good natural light to stage his scenes, consciously differentiating his film from the stagey productions of the competition, Méliès and Pathé. Where he saved on sets, he made up for it with lavish costumes for the characters; Hepworth himself played the frog footman, while his wife took on the roles of the Queen and the White Rabbit. Young May Clark played Alice and the local children (one of whom, Geoffrey Faithfull, went on to become one of Britain's great cinematographers) played the pack of cards who rush towards the camera for the denouement. Even the family dog, Blair, who later rose to fame in *Rescued by Rover* (1905), joins in the throng. Hepworth made good use of trick work in the film, employing some superimposition and clever camerawork to make Alice larger and smaller, and dissolves to 'disappear' the Cheshire cat and turn the Duchess's baby into a pig.

The film was a great success and appeared in the Hepworth catalogue in 1905 and 1906. In fact, it was so popular that individual scenes were issued separately 'to make them more saleable to a few of our more prudent customers'. At this time, film was purchased outright by the exhibitor rather than rented, and to buy the whole film was a major investment. The separate scenes included: the Beautiful Garden, the Duchess and the Pig Baby, the Mad Tea Party and the final Procession of the Cards, and were advertised as being particularly suitable for children's parties. A market for film aimed at children had begun to develop in Britain at this time, with Christmas specials already a feature.

Dir: Percy Stow; **Prod**: Cecil Hepworth; **Prod Co**: Hepworth & Co; **Cast**: May Clark, Cecil M. Hepworth, Margaret Hepworth (Mrs), Norman Whitten.

Ballet mécanique
France, 1924 – 19 mins
Fernand Léger, Dudley Murphy

In the 1920s, a discussion of film and its relationship to other arts and artists began to develop. The emergence of cine clubs and film societies and journals, which were interested in the intersections of film and art, coincided with a variety of modernist movements to produce a heady mix of experimentation. One of the most significant of these is the work/s known as *Ballet mécanique*. It is impossible now to say which came first, the idea for the musical score of *Ballet mécanique* by George Antheil (which was intended to be accompanied by a film) or the film by the well-known artist Fernand Léger and American film-maker Dudley Murphy (which, it was intended, would be accompanied by Antheil's composition). Either way, the two works were conceived together but remained separated until attempts were made to reunite them in recent years. This would always be an uneasy union, as the two pieces had different running times (17 minutes for the film, 30 minutes or so for the score), and Antheil also produced several versions of the score with different instrumentation (originally scored for multiple player-pianos played percussively, xylophones, three aeroplane propellers, an electric bell and a siren). There are also longer and shorter cuts of the film.

To focus on the film – the 17-odd minutes of running time are made up of broadly unrelated images edited together rhythmically, comprising abstract forms, household objects and human figures in repetitive motions, serried ranks of saucepan lids, phallically moving pistons, letters and numbers, Christmas baubles and cake moulds from all angles, with close-ups, fixed or moving, and sometimes broken up with prisms. Striking images of human figures include a close-up of the face of Man Ray's partner, Alice Prin (Kiki of Montparnasse), Dudley Murphy's wife, Katherine, on a swing in a garden and a washerwoman whom Murphy had seen in the street while out with his camera capturing random shots for the film. 'I saw an old washerwoman climbing a flight of stone

Alice Prin (Kiki of Montparnasse) filmed through a prism

stairs ... The scene itself was banal, but by printing it 20 times ... it expressed the futility of life because she never got there.'[1] Murphy inserts his own face into the film briefly, but the final figure is an element introduced by Fernand Léger, an abstract animated Charlie Chaplin, who 'presents' the film.

In terms of contribution to the finished film, Dudley Murphy, who had the most film-making experience, shot the footage using a mix of his own ideas with contributions from Léger, Man Ray and Ezra Pound, and very likely others too. It was planned up to a point. Murphy later said, 'The premise on which we decided to make the film was based on a belief that surprise of image and rhythm would make a pure film without drawing on any of the other arts.'[2] This aligns the film closely with Dadaism and, arguably, with some aspects of Surrealism, as well as incorporating techniques found in abstract animation and pure cinema. The intellectual work of editing the film seems to have been carried out by Léger, and his influence is clearly visible in the choice of figures and household objects etc. which featured frequently in his paintings.

Léger had also had some prior contact with film editing in his study of the montage sequences of Abel Gance's *La Roue* (1922), which impressed him greatly and of which he said, 'The advent of this film is additionally interesting in that it is going to determine a place in the plastic order for an art that has until now remained almost completely descriptive, sentimental, and documentary.'[3] As a study of formal expressiveness and the plastic arts, he could as well have said it of his own film.

Dir: Fernand Léger, Dudley Murphy, with contributions from Man Ray, Ezra Pound; **Separate Musical Score**: George Antheil.

The Battle of the Somme
UK, 1916 – 74 mins
William F. Jury

7.19 a.m. My hand grasped the handle of the camera. I set my teeth. My whole mind was concentrated upon my work. Another thirty seconds passed … I fixed my eyes on the Redoubt. Any second now. Surely it was time. It seemed for me as if I had been turning for hours. Great heavens! Surely it had not misfired. Why doesn't it go up? I looked at my exposure dial … The horrible thought flashed through my mind, that my film might run out before the mine blew. Would it go up before I had time for reload? The thought brought beads of perspiration to my forehead. The agony was awful; indescribable. My hand began to shake. Another 250 feet exposed. I had to keep on. Then it happened.[4]

This is the graphic account given by one of the cameramen, Geoffrey Malins, who filmed the extraordinary *The Battle of the Somme* in June/July 1916. He was shooting the explosion of a massive mine underneath the German trenches on the Western Front that would signal the start of the battle at 7.30 a.m. on 1 July, one of the highlights of the film. His words have a wonderful immediacy, for there is nothing like the eyewitness account, and this is what the people back home must have longed for by the summer of 1916. The film is the real thing but it is also propaganda, not made by the War Office but certainly sanctioned by them. The two cameramen, Malins and John McDowell, another very experienced film-maker, were sent to document General Haig's 'big push' as part of the War Office's new policy to lift the ban on filming at the front and allow the British (and Irish) public to see the preparations and some of the action. It had become essential for the government to be more open about the conduct of the war as they contemplated the implications of conscription, rationing and the expected heavy losses.

It proved the right thing to do. If we find the tone overly 'patriotic' for our tastes, people at the time were grateful for any information at all about what was happening on the front line. At home, in the troop camps and overseas, people went to see the film in their millions. More surprising to the modern audience, accustomed as we are to generic anonymous footage of troops, is that the audience expected to recognise individuals in the film. The intertitles give the names of regiments and battalions in their county and national groupings, the 'Oldham Pals', the Royal Welsh Fusiliers, the Seaforth Highlanders, the Devonshires, for these were principally the volunteer regiments. Recruited together, they were expected to fight well together, but what happened in reality was that they died together, leaving whole communities devastated. As propaganda, the film is subtle, the enemy are not demonised, dead bodies and wounded are not concealed, and if our lads are seen making very free with their canteens and cigarettes for the German prisoners, it is at least a positive message. In terms of truthful film-making, clearly some of the footage is staged, such as the famous 'over the top' sequence, albeit for perfectly good reasons (the camera would have been in the way and the operator too much at risk). There is also a tendency to the 'picturesque', with everlasting lines of troops snaking into the distance, but otherwise it is as real a war film as you will find. It doesn't quite match our image of the Somme – there is no mud to be seen.

Prod: William F. Jury for the British Topical Committee for War Films; **Ph**: Geoffrey Malins, John McDowell; **Ed**: Charles Urban; **Music**: J. Morton Hutcheson (original 1916 medley).

The Battles of Coronel and Falkland Islands
UK, 1927 – 103 mins
Walter Summers

There were various ways to tell a true story in early film – as there are now – from actuality and reportage to the documentary, dramatised documentary or biopic. Historical recreation often crosses the rigid line between fiction and non-fiction. All films relating to historical events have to be staged to a greater or lesser extent, even a 'film of record' such as *The Battle of the Somme**. In the case of *The Battles of Coronel and Falkland Islands*, the cinematic tools used by director Walter Summers to convey reality are a synthesis of documentary technique and fiction devices. His overall intention was to produce a very faithful representation of these two World War I naval battles, the first of which was a triumph for the German Admiral von Spee, who out-thought and outgunned an inferior British force off the coast of Chile at Coronel. The second was a retaliatory strike by ace British tactician Admiral Fisher, who sent two new battle cruisers, *Invincible* and *Inflexible*, to the South Atlantic under Vice-Admiral Sturdee to restore British pride and supremacy. The battles, which took place early in the war, were significant in establishing a stalemate between the navies, although the law of unintended consequences led the Germans to switch tactics to commerce-raiding through the U-boat campaign, which became a very serious threat to the British line of supply.

The film portrays a noble defeat and a notable British victory but it is not propaganda per se, being made so long after the fact; in part it was a response to a German film called *Unsere Emden* (1926) about a previous naval incident of the Great War, which had an almost identical treatment – a very accurate, detailed account, made with the support of the German Admiralty and exhibiting a detached perspective which maintained scrupulous fairness in its treatment of the British enemy. Summers's polite one-upmanship was *almost* as respectful to the Germans. Powell and Pressburger's *Battle of the River Plate* (1956) followed in this tradition after an almost identical naval confrontation in the South Atlantic during World War II and featuring, appropriately, the German battleship *Graf Von Spee*, named after the renowned admiral.

It is curious that the film is not better known today, for the film-making is astonishingly effective, leading critic C. A. Lejeune to comment, '*The Battles of Coronel and Falkland Islands* is without question the best motion picture that a British director has ever made.'[5] She also mentioned it in the same breath as *Metropolis** and Abel Gance's *La Roue* (1922), and it was, inevitably, compared to *Battleship Potemkin**. Walter Summers's film-making style, like Eisenstein's, glories in the beauty of the machine – the diagonals of the big guns, the vast scale of the battleships, the fierce industry of the shipyards, the rhythm of feet on the gangplank, the movement of men shovelling coal as the needle on a pressure gauge mounts, the reflected gleam of water on the cabin walls – but unlike *Potemkin*, it is devoid of symbolism. The real influence of *Potemkin* on this film, I suspect, is the extreme precision with which it was made. Summers raised his game, using editing techniques more commonly found in fiction film, to condense time and add character and mood to particular sequences in the story. The photography, composition, lighting and pacing are masterly. But it also has a strong documentary impulse, with detailed research and real locations (or the next best thing – St Mary's in the Isles of Scilly is a remarkably good fit for Port Stanley in the Falklands); most impressively, perhaps, to a modern audience is his realised ambition to use real ships, with the co-operation of the Admiralty. They are the stars of the show and significantly, in the surviving print, are credited, whereas the actors are not.

Dir: Walter Summers; **Scr**: John Buchan, Harry Engholm, Frank C. Bowen; **Ph**: Jack Parker, Stanley Rodwell, E. E. Warneford.

The Battleship Potemkin (*Bronenosets Potyomkin*)
USSR, 1925 – 70 mins
Sergei M. Eisenstein

The Battleship Potemkin is arguably the most celebrated silent film of all. Because it has acquired so much critical baggage, it can seem a bit daunting to the uninitiated. My advice, if you are in the happy position of not having seen it, is not to read anything about the film and just watch it, uncluttered by the arguments of theorists or historians. This is, above all, a great action movie. Make sure you see a restored copy, as many previously distributed versions were cut, particularly the more gruesome scenes (such as the snarling face of a Cossack as he brings his sabre slashing across the old woman's face in the Odessa steps sequence).

The action starts aboard the battleship at anchor off Odessa on the Black Sea and it's a grabber. A title appears, 'Part I, The Men and the Maggots'. Two sailors conclude a secret meeting in the ship's rigging by declaring their support for the workers' uprising against the tsarist regime. The spark that leads the sailors to mutiny is the discovery that their meat is rotten and crawling with maggots, a metaphor for the corruption of the chain of command. A showdown with the captain ensues. He brings in the marines when they refuse to take orders. As the marines prepare to fire, the leader of the mutinous sailors, Vakulinchuk, calls to them, 'Brothers!', and the marines lower their rifles refusing to fire on their comrades. The officers are soon overwhelmed and the revolutionaries victorious. When the hero of the hour is himself killed, however, his dead body is taken ashore and becomes the focus around which the people and the sailors join forces. There is a joyful moment in which the people of Odessa organise a spontaneous flotilla of sailing boats to take food over to the ship for the sailors as other citizens look on from the steps mounting the hill; all seems harmonious before the inevitable backlash descends. That descent is the most famous scene in film history, the massacre on the Odessa steps. Ranks of troops shoot volleys of rifle fire into the crowd, a child is trampled as they flee and is borne towards the soldiers by its mother, who attempts to stop them firing, but they are merciless and gun her down. Another mother is shot and, in falling, pushes her baby's pram down the steps to looks of horror from the crowd who are being hacked to pieces by mounted Cossacks. It appears that the same fate will befall the sailors of the *Potemkin* as they are faced with the long guns of the entire Black Sea fleet. But as

Poster for Eisenstein's *Battleship Potemkin*

Eisenstein himself said, 'The task of a film about 1905 is grounded in upbeat mood, not a mournful one, because our assessment of all the events of that year is definitely in the major key.'[6] The *Potemkin* is let by in an act of comradeship.

Nowadays, we talk about *Battleship Potemkin* almost exclusively in terms of its technical achievements, perhaps because Eisenstein wrote so much about his film-making theory, the 'montage of attractions'; this may, however, underestimate his interest in the content and the message rather than the means of telling it. *Potemkin* is constructed very like his film *Stachka** (made in the same year): that is, broken up into episodes that were clearly already familiar incidents to his potential audience. But the popular appeal was undermined by the fact that despite being specifically commissioned to celebrate the anniversary of the Revolution, the film failed to find that broad popular audience, as it was only released in second-run houses after its glitzy premiere in the Bolshoi Theatre. After some persuasion, however, Sovkino released the film in Germany, from where its fame spread with astonishing rapidity. The total integration of film-making technique with its message, with its subdued performance style and stunning actions sequences, was immediately recognised by film-makers and critics in the West, who hailed it as a masterpiece, and it is.

Dir: Sergei M. Eisenstein; **Co-dir**: Grigori Aleksandrov; **Ph**: Eduard Tisse; **Cast**: Vladimir Barsky, Aleksandr Antonov, Grigori V. Aleksandrov, Mikhail Gomorov.

Beggars of Life
US, 1928 – 82 mins
William Wellman

Contemporary critics were generally unimpressed by this picture, which is an object lesson in the distorting lens of history. Essentially the romance of a couple of down-on-their-luck youngsters on the run from the law who fall in with a crowd of hoboes hopping freight trains, it appeals to the modern audience more perhaps because of what happened long after its release. One was the rise of Louise Brooks to the pantheon of iconic movie stars, while the other was the emergence of classical Hollywood narrative.

The story and structure feel recognisable to us – we understand how the relationship between the two protagonists will go; we understand that foster fathers are generally abusive; we know that Louise Brooks in man's clothes is going to be even cuter than she is already and that the coarse, brutish Wallace Beery will turn out to be a saint. What is more, even though the film works perfectly as a silent, it was in fact made as a part-talkie (allegedly, it was during the filming of *Beggars of Life* that the boom mic was first used). I'm not sure how this contributes to the feeling of it being a later American film but that *is* what it feels like. Of course, we are familiar with the hobo genre in a way that contemporary commentators could not have been, and that also reinforces our association with the Depression and the 1930s. Seen in terms of Louise Brooks's career, *Beggars of Life* feels so familiarly 'Hollywood', whereas *Pandora's Box** feels so much a part of old European silent style that it requires a double take to realise that *Pandora's Box* was actually made later. It seems all wrong somehow.

But perhaps, for once, we might allow ourselves to be grateful for the distorting lens, for this is a film to wallow in – yes, it *is* unrealistic and it *is* sentimental, but it is so charming and beautiful, and the characters so endearing, that we are all delighted to forgive it any such minor faults. Louise Brooks is a really good actress and gets to show it, while

Richard Arlen and Louise Brooks on the run as hoboes

Wallace Beery, having burst onto the screen like a stage pirate, gives a performance that becomes progressively more subtle and sensitive as the film moves along. There are also some very fine film-making moments, such as the whole opening sequence in which Richard Arlen's hungry young drifter smells breakfast and walks into a bright kitchen to beg for food, only to realise with a jolt that the man sitting in front of the ham and eggs is dead. That contrast is superb and leads straight into his introduction to the girl, who explains why she has killed the farmer. As she tells her story, a close-up of her face is superimposed over images of the lust-ridden farmer's attack, which led her to pull the shotgun on him. Most famous is the scene that same night, when the young drifter, having taken her under his wing, makes a bed for them in a hayrick. They are thrown into close proximity, which given her recent experience might be cause for uneasiness, but as they talk of a home they can each only aspire to, it is clear already that this is love of an innocent but immutable kind. The best line of the movie is given to its star (Wallace Beery that is, not Louise Brooks) as, despite his own desires to carry the girl away, he realises the fact of their love for each other, 'I've heard about it. But I've never seen it before.' You can hear him saying it, even though it's only an intertitle.

Dir: William Wellman; **Ph**: Henry Gerrard; **Scr**: Benjamin Glazer; **Cast**: Wallace Beery, Louise Brooks, Richard Arlen.

Berlin, Symphony of a City (Berlin, die Sinfonie der Großstadt)

Germany, 1927 – 65 mins
Walter Ruttmann

We are so used to being situated neatly in a city by the sight of an iconic building (New York/Empire State Building, Paris/Eiffel Tower, Big Ben/London) that the opening of this time-motion study of a day in the life of Berlin comes as something of surprise (I don't think the Brandenburg Gate even makes an appearance).

The opening is truly inspired, however. We start serenely with an image of water and overlaid abstract patterning reminiscent of Ruttmann's earlier experimental films. Lines represent the waves on the water, a semicircle the rising sun; the lines break upwards and are cut into a match shot of the gates of a level crossing rising to let through a thundering steam train. Cutting rapidly between telegraph poles, racing wheels and pumping pistons, we rush past the country, the suburbs, the industrial hinterland, then the housing estates and advertising hoardings of the great city to arrive at Anhalter Bahnhof (Berlin's gateway to the south). As the train slows and the music swells, we see a vista of the city from above, and cutting from building to building, we finally settle on a clock tower – 5 o'clock! Like Cavalcanti's *Rien que les heures* (1926), the organising principle is temporal – it settles into the five 'acts' characteristic of the symphony, during which we see the city in all its aspects from dawn to dusk. These acts all have a slightly different 'feel', if not as clearly defined as a tempo in musical terms. The empty streets and opening up of gates, solitary cats on cobbled streets and slowly building pressure of steam engines that will power the wheels of industry give way to the final movement: the bright lights and entertainments, glamorous or sleazy, of the city at night.

The style of the film is part of the art deco aesthetic of which Ruttmann was a leading proponent. He makes much use of special effects, including multiple exposures and prisms to fracture the images, to name but two. He is also influenced by Vertov's shooting and cutting style, with consistently changing angles, points of view and focal planes, although this kinetic activity is more architectural in Ruttmann's case. A street of moving traffic, for example, will show trams from ground level and from overhead, from the front or coming straight towards the screen, crossing bottom left to top right, followed by a reverse diagonal, or through an elevated bridge from below. The tempo of the cutting is deliberate and is reflected in Meisel's original orchestral score, which contains some subtle impressionistic sound effects. This was as far as Ruttmann was ready to go in integrating sound and image, as he was very aware of the potential difficulties of that process. The choice of traditional orchestral score enables the film to be both documentary and art.

But the film is full of elements that don't quite fit. Filmed over a year in order to capture images without the subjects' knowledge, there are nevertheless several staged scenes – the close-up face of a suicide (very reminiscent of Eisenstein) and an interior of a cinema showing Chaplin's feet in *The Gold Rush**. The film occasionally juxtaposes shots for effect (for example, the legs of the workers going into the factory with the legs of cattle herded into the dairy), but generally this is an aesthetic choice – because they look similar and because of the shapes they make – rather than a social comment. This objectification of humankind was a feature of German film (see also *The Oyster Princess**) deriving from theatre design.

Dir: Walter Ruttmann; **Scr**: Karl Freund and Walter Ruttmann, based on an idea by Carl Mayer; **Ph**: Karl Freund; **Special Musical Score**: Edmund Meisel.

The Big Swallow
UK, 1901 – 1 min.
James Williamson

It is difficult to select examples from the early days of film that can stand alongside the great creative works of late-1920s cinema. It is not enough simply to be a 'first', which is why I have chosen this example from British film pioneer James Williamson, who had a real knack for understanding the audience's point of view and then playing with the form. It is a film that is simple but perfectly satisfying and leaves one with a nice little puzzle to think about. The plot is explained in Williamson's own catalogue description:

> 'I won't! I won't! I'll eat the camera first.' Gentleman reading, finds a camera fiend with his head under a cloth, focusing him up. He orders him off, approaching nearer and nearer, gesticulating and ordering the photographer off, until his head fills the picture, and finally his mouth only occupies the screen. He opens it, and first the camera, and then the operator disappear inside. He retires munching him up and expressing his great satisfaction.

The big close-up of the man's mouth as it engulfs the entire frame has become one of the iconic images of the cinema. It is also, incidentally, reminiscent of the 'Hell's Mouth', an image going back to the Middle Ages, commonly used in religious imagery and employed extensively since as a device in theatre. The character of the 'camera fiend' was a more contemporary figure, born out of the introduction of the cheap Kodak camera in the 1880s. These overenthusiastic snappers were, no doubt, a considerable nuisance to those who didn't want their privacy invaded, but the comic possibilities were taken up by film-makers, cartoonists and, later, postcard illustrators. The man takes instant revenge, walking towards the camera (we are currently seeing as if through the cameraman's eyes) into bigger and bigger close-up till his mouth opens and consumes it). We see the camera and cameraman fall into the mouth, which provides the core of the joke – how can we be seeing what we are seeing if the camera has fallen into this dark void? Then, even more bizarrely, we pull back to our previous point of view of the man in close-up, swallowing and licking his lips. This should occupy no more of anyone's time than the notion of 'infinity plus one', but it does demonstrate a facility to manipulate the internal logic of the cinema's properties.

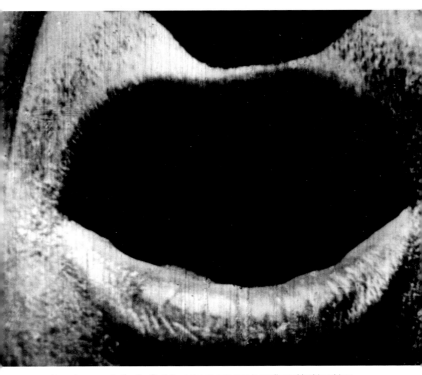

An early moment of self-reflexivity as the cameraman is swallowed by his subject

As stated above, Williamson had a talent for continuity, virtually inventing continuity editing in his film of the same year, *Fire!* In this, a policeman who discovers a furiously burning building races out of shot and is matched running into the next shot to alert the men at the fire station. Cutting on action is a form of film grammar that we now take for granted. Here is a genuine YouTube comment from a confused teenager:

> 'The Big Swallow' is a very clever and artful, if a little disturbing and surreal at the same time, piece of early film history. Unfortunately, because it didn't originally have narration to explain what was going on (this was added later, or was narrated by someone standing behind the audience in public viewings), I can't imagine it made much sense, even if it's cool to watch.

Even though one wonders what there was to explain (the 'plot' wouldn't confuse a three-year-old), the essential point is made even a century or more on – it is 'cool to watch'.

Dir: James Williamson; **Cast**: Sam Dalton.

The Birth of a Flower
GB, 1910 – 8 mins
F. Percy Smith

The Birth of a Flower has been in continuous distribution since it was
released in 1910. This is unusual, particularly in a market (science and
nature film) that thrives on improving on past productions. Take a look
on the ubiquitous YouTube and you will see many examples of time-lapse
openings of flowers, but in a hundred years almost nothing has changed
technically – natural colour as opposed to tinting is about the only real
improvement – which may explain the longevity of Percy Smith's
innovative film. The experience of watching flowers open still has a
balletic and slightly hypnotic quality that we find pleasurable, and the
film's simple movement lends itself well to music and is much favoured
by silent film composers. The great producer Charles Urban, who had
discovered Smith languishing at the Educational Board, took him on and
gave him the autonomy to do what he did best. The investment paid off
and expensive colour prints of the film were produced, initially with
tinting and later in Urban's own process, Kinemacolor. The parallels with
the treatment given to nature film today are striking. If you take the
careers of the two biggest names in British nature film – Percy Smith and
David Attenborough – there is a continuity of excellence that stretches
from the dawn of cinema to the digital age.

The film's creator, Frank Percy Smith (1880–1945), was a true
pioneer, who invented original methods for taking time-lapse film and
micro-cinematography, involving all kinds of 'Heath Robinson'
home-made devices, including the installation of alarms in his suburban
London home to wake him up in the middle of the night if the film in
the camera needed changing. Endlessly patient, like all the best
naturalists, he could take up to two and a half years to complete a film.
But these were not delivered in a dry scientific manner. Smith also had
the popular touch, with the happy knack (as he put it himself) of being
able to feed his audience 'the powder of instruction in the jam of

entertainment'. His films of balancing bluebottles and acrobatic flies are both entertaining and mildly instructional. *Birth of a Flower*, however, is presented very straight, with almost no comment – and none is necessary – apart from a title naming the flowers under observation and the time that they took to open, so that the audience could marvel at the speed made possible by the stop-motion filming. Flowers are presented in a front-on view on a table and photographed about once a minute so that we see blooming in succession: hyacinths, crocuses, snowdrops, Neapolitan onion flowers, narcissi, Japanese lilies, garden anemones and roses. Audiences, according to the contemporary trade press, would burst into spontaneous applause and demand that the film be shown again. Even today's sophisticated viewers often let out an audible gasp when the film is screened.

Dir: F. Percy Smith; **Prod Co**: Kineto/Urban Science Series; **Prod**: Charles Urban.

The Birth of a Nation
US, 1915 – 191 mins
D. W. Griffith

D. W. Griffith's *The Birth of a Nation* was huge, in every sense. It was the first great blockbuster of the American cinema, taking unprecedented box office and road-shown for over a decade in the biggest theatres at ticket prices normally associated only with the most lavish productions of the legitimate theatre. *The Birth of a Nation* phenomenon was indeed all about theatre, for Griffith, despite a successful seven-year career at the Biograph studios, had always had aspirations towards the stage. This led him to take advantage of a property that suddenly became available – at a crucial point when the nation was celebrating the fiftieth anniversary of the end of the Civil War – a popular play about the ante-bellum 'Reconstruction' of the South, Thomas Dixon's *The Clansman*. As a Southerner himself, Griffith was drawn to a story that is now difficult for modern audiences to watch because of its racist content. The play and its source novels concern the imposition by the victorious Abolitionists on the defeated Confederacy of a vengeful, corrupt and incompetent black leadership that would disenfranchise the whites and allow intermarriage between the races. This, and fear of the rape of their women, leads to the rise of the Ku Klux Klan, who ride heroically to the rescue.

Griffith kept close to the play but added a prologue (effectively the entire first half of the film), supplying a Civil War backstory (he had specialised in Civil War dramas for some years) which justified the concept of the Nation's birth. This related the stories of two intertwined families, one Northern, one Southern, along with the added exposition of the Abolitionist, who, unduly influenced by his mulatto mistress, will set the former slave free to cause havoc and ultimately the assassination of President Lincoln, the last hope of the South. This prologue gives the film its epic scope and establishes our sympathy with a set of characters, particularly the 'Little Colonel' played by Henry B. Walthall, who in the second half of the movie establishes the Clan and rides to the rescue accompanied by the soaring chords of Wagner's *Ride of the Valkyries*.

The sense that our sympathy for the characters is being manipulated makes it difficult for the modern audience to uncouple the film from unavoidable associations with Nazism and see the appeal of the narrative with 1915 eyes. Conversely, the representation of the African-Americans was so offensive that it led to riots and widespread condemnation even at the time. Clearly, though, there was something about the ambition and scope of this melodrama that overrode these objections. It is often said that the film's success was due to technical innovation and carefully nurtured performance, but I think these factors, good as they are (particularly the battle scenes), maybe less important than the presentation the film was given on release. It is significant that the title was changed shortly after it was first shown, from 'The Clansman' to the all-encompassing 'Birth of a Nation'. It is significant that the film's titles contain a strong anti-war message, 'Dare we dream of a golden day when the bestial war will rule no more'. It is significant that every intertitle frame carries Griffith's name and that his opening disclaimer ranks the work with the Bible and Shakespeare. It is significant, especially, that he quotes (albeit inaccurately) the President of the United States in the year of release, Woodrow Wilson, a Southerner and a fierce segregationist, recently re-elected on the ticket that kept the US out of the war raging in Europe, who, unsurprisingly, loved Griffith's film, describing it as resembling 'history written by lightning'. Despite the arrogance and hyperbole, the racism and inaccurate rendering of history, this film deserves to be understood for its subsequent colossal influence on the film industry.

Dir: D. W. Griffith; **Scr**: D. W. Griffith, Frank E. Wood, from the book and play by Thomas F. Dixon Jr; **Ph**: Billy Bitzer; **Cast**: Henry B. Walthall, Mae Marsh, Lillian Gish, Robert Harron, Mary Alden.

Blackmail
UK, 1929 – 82 mins
Alfred Hitchcock

Hitchcock's silent *Blackmail* is one of, if not *the*, best British films of the late 1920s. Made in 1929, during the transition to the sound picture, the film was commissioned as a silent film and also as a part-talkie with music and some dialogue scenes. It nicely illustrates the problems faced by the producers during the tricky transitional period – these were not so much technical (although those were bad enough) but because producers and the public had difficulty conceiving *how* pictures with sound would work. Margaret Kennedy, in her essay *The Mechanised Muse*, describes the difficulty this innovation posed for film-makers:

> Science was offering a wonderful baby, a Midas, an infant Hercules, to anyone who could improvise a cradle large enough to hold it … Caveman, shepherd and peasant – each had his own rough, primitive idea of what a satisfactory drawing or tune or play should be. As much could *not* be said, of the first fabricators of sound films. They had no notion of what they wanted to make. Nor had the public much notion of what it wanted to see and hear. The artist and audience were equally at a loss.[7]

Enter young(ish) Alfred Hitchcock, who managed to simultaneously produce a beautifully crafted silent film *and* a sound version, tackling the considerable technical obstacles of adding dialogue with such an imaginative and intelligent approach that it has become more famous for this aspect of its composition than for its quality as a film. Many people are completely unaware of the silent version, despite the fact that it is superior to the sound version in several ways – it contains more shots, more camera movement and, through the fluidity of the cutting, conveys the narrative with greater style. Not that the sound version is bad – in fact, it was exceptionally good for the year, and contains a couple of innovations, such as the famous 'shock cut' in which a woman's scream carries over the cut from Alice's view of what looks like a knifed body to the landlady's discovery of the murdered artist's corpse; but the dialogue sequences are nevertheless jarring and unbalance the flow of the film. As a silent film, however, it is very, very good: every shot is packed with significance, moving the story inexorably on.

Dozens of documentaries on Hitchcock pick out the legendary 'knife' scene, but as an illustration of the film-maker's skill, just look at the first 7 minutes of the film, from the close-up of the wheel of the flying-squad van to the cell door slamming shut on the villain they have set out to arrest. The composition, the choice of angle, the low-key lighting, set

Hitchcock's terror of policemen drives the narrative of *Blackmail*

design and the detail of each shot is astounding: the villain watches the policemen steal up to the door sideways in a mirror; simultaneously, they see the villain's hand creeping towards his gun as a silhouette on the wall, with the reverse shot showing their faces shadowed by the slats of the bedroom blind. The effect is of consummate cleverness, although the story itself is simple – a lively young girl engaged to a rather stuffy policeman boyfriend is enticed up to an artist's studio and there stabs him to death to avoid what we might now call date-rape.

The consequences of her actions play out with mounting tension in more or less real time (which creates the suspense), as her copper boyfriend plays cat and mouse with an opportunistic blackmailer to save her from the awful fate that befell the villain in the opening minutes. In the final reel, Hitchcock sets up the first of the famous set-piece chases – in this case, over the iconic dome of the British Museum – that would become his trademark.

Dir: Alfred Hitchcock; **Scr**: Alfred Hitchcock, Garnett Weston, Charles Bennett (from his play); **Ph**: Jack Cox; **Cast**: Anny Ondra, John Longden, Cyril Ritchard, Donald Calthrop, Sara Allgood, Charles Paton.

Body and Soul
US, 1925 – 102 mins
Oscar Micheaux

Oscar Micheaux is the only black director who has come down to us
from the silent period that even the most enthusiastic silent film fan
could name, and is therefore worthy of some attention.

Micheaux, a very driven man who had been a successful farmer and a
writer, set up his own independent production company to produce
films with an all-black cast. These were mostly shown only to African-
American audiences and are consequently known as 'race films'.

Of these, *Within Our Gates* (1920) and *Body and Soul* are the two
best-known examples. The first is a response to the kind of racist
portrayal of African-Americans found in *Birth of a Nation**, while the
second is a critique of the power of corrupt preachers, and is also
notable for the screen debut of Paul Robeson, the first African-American
actor to achieve international star status.

In a very comprehensive article in *Oscar Micheaux and His Circle:
African American Filmmaking and Race Cinema in the Silent Era*,[8] Charles
Musser traces the origins of the film to three race plays written by white
playwrights, *The Emperor Jones* and *All God's Chillun' Got Wings* by
Eugene O'Neill, and *Roseanne* by Nan Bagby Stephens. According to his
thesis, the construction and content of these plays help to unpack the
unusual structure of *Body and Soul*, which presents a very substantial
part of the film's action as a dream in flashback by the central character,
Martha Jane, who falls under the influence of a convict posing as a
charismatic preacher. It partially explains the malevolent character played
by Robeson – who delivers an electrifying turn as the preacher whipping
the congregation into a religious frenzy – and the inability of Martha
Jane's daughter, Isabelle, to confess to her mother that she has been
raped by the preacher, who has, moreover, forced her to take the blame
for the theft of her mother's money which she has been putting aside for
her daughter's marriage.

It is revealed that the evil consequences of Martha's indulgence of the false preacher are contained within a dream, which makes sense in the context of the three influential plays but comes as a surprise to the modern viewer, for whom the dream motif is overfamiliar and generally regarded as a cop-out. However, as Musser explains, the device of the dream plays to the African-American psyche, in which life in a racist world can be seen as a waking nightmare and the reason for the self-destructive behaviour of figures like Isabelle, who runs away to starve in a city garret because she knows no one will believe her. It may be difficult for contemporary audiences to understand Micheaux's dramas without this context, but even so, *Body and Soul* is a compelling drama lifted by the acting, particularly by Robeson, who also plays a dual role as Isabelle's honest fiancé, Sylvester. In this case, it is worth reading some of the background *before* seeing the movie.

Dir: Oscar Micheaux; **Scr**: Oscar Micheaux (from his novel); **Cast**: Paul Robeson, Mercedes Gilbert, Julia Theresa Russell, Lawrence Chenault.

The Cabinet of Dr. Caligari (*Das Cabinet des Dr. Caligari*)
Germany, 1920 – 72 mins
Robert Wiene

If you had to pick a top ten of silent films in terms of innovation, uniqueness and influence, then *The Cabinet of Dr. Caligari* would be on it. *Caligari* was the first self-conscious art film, the herald of the short-lived but significant Expressionist movement in postwar German film and, moreover, continues to appeal to modern audiences because of its 'look', its themes and its affinity with the later horror movie. Some of that affinity comes from the ghost-story tradition: for example, the film has a framing device which was common in the written form, whose function is to ease us into a story that threatens to be unsettling with the promise that we will be retrieved from it in the end. This type of narrative device was also popular in theatrical traditions of the period such as Grand Guignol. The plot is familiar too for a modern audience – it's a horror film with a mad scientist, the evil Dr Caligari, his pitiable monster, Cesare the somnambulist, and, of course, the vulnerable young girl and vengeful hero. There is a twist, however, in that the final moments and closing of our framing story do not bring us back to the comfort of the garden bench where we started but instead hurl us into an insane asylum where the evil doctor has become the director and all the characters are the inmates. Again, this kind of surprise ending was something of a convention, certainly of Grand Guignol.

The structure of the film is accessible, with straightforward continuity editing. The camera is static and positioned front on, again recalling the theatre, and this is emphasised by the feature for which the film is most famous, its sets. These are principally 'flats', painted in the Expressionist art style that had become fashionable by this time. With distorted perspectives, steep angles and hand-drawn backdrops evoking the streets of medieval *Mitteleuropa*, the flats are set upstage/downstage in the proscenium frame making no effort at realism, unlike later, more

Conrad Veidt's body language reflects the angular set design

expensive 'Expressionist' films (*Metropolis**, *The Golem**) where the life-size sets were built in three dimensions. The costumes, too, belong to no particular time, evoking stock characters of theatrical productions. They are effective, though, and complemented by the grotesque make-up. The acting style is splendidly pantomimic and particularly brilliant from Werner Krauss as Caligari and Conrad Veidt as Cesare, who both adopt particularly expressive movements. Caligari scuttles rapidly in tiny steps like some horrid insect, while Cesare incorporates himself into the nightmarish sets in the posture of a dancer, the use of close-ups allowing both figures to conjure up evil and pathos.

All the elements of the film combine so well to signify the obsessive unbalanced mind that, while one (always) sympathises with the writers, it is difficult to imagine a better ending, and despite the clash of egos that has characterised debate about his film since its release (the writers Carl Mayer and Hans Janowitz complained that it softened the anti-authoritarian message; Kracauer thought it was indicative of the state of mind of the entire German nation), I think Wiene had it right.

Dir: Robert Wiene; **Scr**: Carl Mayer, Hans Janowitz; **Ph**: Willy Hameister; **Art Dir**: Hermann Warm, Walter Reimann, Walter Röhrig; **Cast**: Conrad Veidt, Werner Krauss, Lil Dagover.

Cabiria
Italy, 1914 – 180 mins
Giovanni Pastrone

'Who now shall sing of the Punic Wars? Who shall remember Capua and Metaurus, Utica and Zana?' intones the romantic poet Gabriele d'Annunzio in the final intertitle of this epic film. Well, quite. Few of us today will be as familiar with the names and events of third-century Roman history as audiences were in the Italy of 1913. (My advice: if you are going to invest three hours of your life viewing *Cabiria*, then get the best out of it by spending ten minutes looking up the details of the second Punic War.) Broadly, the Romans are fighting the Carthaginians. A Roman girl child, Cabiria, becomes separated from her parents when Etna erupts, is kidnapped by pirates, destined as a sacrifice to Moloch in Carthage and is eventually rescued by the Roman Fulvio Axilla and his strongman slave Maciste. On the way, we meet Roman consuls Marcellus and Scipio, their enemy Hannibal, the mercenary King Massinissa, Archimedes and the lusty princess Sofonisba.

It's a cracking story but not always elegantly conveyed. The events are recounted in autonomous scenes, in chronological succession, with forward-facing intertitles that tell you what you are about to see. There is no editing or parallel action, and in this respect *Cabiria* feels slightly old-fashioned. More effective ways of telling a story were clearly already in circulation; however, this 'tableaux' approach probably reflects the pictorialist conventions of delivering classical tales of the time, as well as the style of classical literary sources, which tended to be episodic. Old-fashioned or not, Giovanni Pastrone went one better than earlier renderings of classical stories by scaling up massively. Arising out of the trend for 'film d'art' adaptations of classic works, a precedent had been set in Italy in 1911 by *L'Inferno*, which not only had a much longer running time than most films but employed more lavish set design and special effects. In *Cabiria*, the sets were huge, the story huge in scope and included an equally huge individual, Maciste, whose character became so popular it spawned a franchise. It was, in effect, an epic and though not unique, the substantial marketing campaign that accompanied its release in 1914 made it uniquely influential. It directly influenced D. W. Griffith's *Intolerance* (1916) and in the longer term, of course, the epic film would go on to become a whole genre of its own.

A number of other features of *Cabiria* were taken up by various film-makers – most notably the use of camera movement to compensate for the fixed point of view and the distance of the viewer from the action necessitated by the large sets. The 'Cabiria' movement, as it was referred to by American cameramen, was a slow diagonal track in and out which took you closer to the rather small figures. Pastrone also worked in up to five planes of action, so that there is always movement in foreground, middle ground and background to enhance the sense of three-dimensionality. This was a favoured technique, particularly of the Pathé cameramen during the 1900s, who were working to a nineteenth-century photographic ideal. Some of the effects are good: in particular, Sofonisba's nightmare, in which great staring eyes appear as if in her mind, courtesy of Segundo de Chomón, a master of film matte work. The set pieces are fabulous and there is a lot of fire: from the eruption of the volcano, to Moloch's fiery pit, into which the naked Cabiria is to be flung, to the burning of the Roman fleet by Archimedes.
Although Pastrone tries to create heroic characters in the shape of Fulvio and Maciste, who will take us through the great historical events unfolding, the framing prevents us from getting close enough to the story to create any emotion other than wonder at its magnitude.

Dir/Scr: Giovanni Pastrone; **Ph**: Augusto Battagliotti, Eugenio Bava, Natale Chiusano, Giovanni Tomatis, Carlo Franzeri; **Cast**: Lydia Quaranta, Bartolomeo Pagano, Umberto Mozzato, Italia Almirante Manzini, Raffaele di Napoli, Dante Testa.

The Cameraman's Revenge
(Mest' kinematografičeskogo operatora)
Russia, 1912 – 13 mins
Ladislas Starewicz

Transformations of scale and magnitude are a chief delight of the
cinema, in its capacity as successor and appropriator of ancient
entertainments such as the flea circus that have bemused and fascinated
audiences for generations. These shows relied on meticulous modelling
(they were developed originally by watchmakers) and showmanship but
also on a conspiracy not just between showman and spectator but
particularly between adults and children. Perhaps the cat is now out of
the bag, but the question 'are flea circuses real' is still frequently asked
today on internet Q&A sites. Both kids and adults are fascinated by tiny
things, so puppet animation has a natural appeal, something Ladislaw
Starewicz was aware of a century ago in Russia when he began making
his animated insect films. Details about his methods are still hard to come
by today, with most sources plumping for dead insect carapaces and
sealing wax articulated with wire. Reports in the London press on the
release of his first film, a medieval romance called *The Beautiful
Leukanida* (1912), kept up the pretence that the insects were alive and
trained by some clever Russian scientist, adding to the sense of wonder
at the scarcely believable detail and realistic movement of their bodies.

The same year, Starewicz released *The Cameraman's Revenge*, which
has the rather more adult theme of marital infidelity in a bourgeois
household. So, added to our astonishment at the articulation of the
insect characters is surprise at the story, which is a little risqué.
The principal characters are Mr and Mrs Beetle, who live outside of town
and are a little bored. Mr Beetle goes into town regularly in search of
excitement and meets an exotic dragonfly at a nightclub. In winning the
affections of the dragonfly dancer, he fights off a rival suitor, the
grasshopper, who turns out to be a cameraman and in revenge decides
to follow the adulterous pair and secretly film them. At the 'Hotel

d'Amour', he films them through the keyhole – reminiscent of those very early voyeuristic films. Mrs Beetle also has a paramour whom she is seeing behind her husband's back – a romantic artist who is painting her portrait. She is caught in flagrante by her husband, who ejects the artist violently but forgives his wife, and takes her off to the movies. At the open-air cinema the vengeful grasshopper shows the incriminating film to Mr Beetle's wife with predictable results – Mrs Beetle kicks her husband through the cinema screen, Mr Beetle lays into the grasshopper and they end up in jail, where they have time to reflect on their behaviour.

Apart from the moral story and the beautiful animation (there is an especially graceful movement when the grasshopper lifts the dragonfly dancer down from the stage), and apart from the reflexive pleasures of seeing such an early reference to film and the cinema, what impresses most (as always in animation and particularly in the work of the lone genius) is the 'unnecessary' detail. When we know how much labour goes into the movement of the characters and the building of the models, it is incomprehensible why the film-maker would make life harder for himself by introducing extra characters like the beetle servant who bustles about fetching and carrying and building the sitting-room fire, or add the wobble in the turn of the wheel of the motorcar as it sets off. But, of course, that is the secret of the flea circus.

Dir/Scr/Ph/Anim: Ladislas Starewicz.

Casanova
France, 1927 – 132 mins
Alexandre Volkoff

If I wanted to persuade a male of the species to develop an interest in
silent cinema, I would show him a movie with Buster Keaton; if I wanted
to persuade a female, then I think I might choose a film starring the
great Russian actor Ivan Mosjoukine. Beside the other great romantic
leads of the silent era, Valentino or Fairbanks, he is not so well known
today, but he should be. Not as conventionally handsome perhaps, but
with charisma in spades and a famously piercing gaze, Mosjoukine was
loved by the camera. He had a great range of physical expressions, from
the minutest registering of emotion to the most grandiose theatrical
gesturing. It was appropriate that he was cast as Edmund Kean, the
great Shakespearian actor, but also that he played the role of Casanova,
whose appeal required a more intimate approach. As with many stars,
the star persona transcends the body of films in which they appear, so
that it can be difficult to choose a representative example. I could as
easily have chosen *Kean* (1924) or the dazzling *Michel Strogoff* (1926),
or any of the other big features he made with his fellow émigré Russian
film-makers in 1920s Paris. He also had an interest in the surrealist style
and displayed a talent for absurdist comedy, as in the delightfully odd *Le
Brasier ardent* (1923). *Casanova* shows none of this experimental
tendency, however, and is a straightforward historical romp.

From the opening sequence with its firework spectacular, this film is
an exercise in ebullience. It was shot partially in Venice, where most of
the action takes place, and is one of the film's principal pleasures; the
other location is a simulated St Petersburg, ably rendered by talented art
director Noë Bloch and costume designer Boris Bilinsky. Added to this are
two Pathécolor sequences: the grand ball at the court of Catherine the
Great and the final carnival scene, in which a sense of real
sumptuousness is created by the settings and costumes. The opulence is
enhanced by a good deal of frenzied movement – our hero, when not

The charismatic Ivan Mosjoukine as 'the great lover' in suitably opulent surroundings

making love to women, is forever jumping in and out of windows, running over rooftops and fighting with swords.

When we first meet Casanova, it is 'the morning after the night before', and he is awakened by two pretty blonde maids who attend to his every whim, a pair of puppies reflecting their charms – all is lightness luxury and laughter. When the inevitable creditor arrives with the bailiffs, his intrusive search for possessions reveals the famous courtesan and dancer, Corticelli, in Casanova's bed. The bawdiness continues with the famous Dance of the Swords scene, in which Corticelli and her dancers perform a strip dance using (with no subtle symbolism) the gentlemen's swords, and although we only see the dance in silhouette, when Casanova bears the naked Corticelli from the floor, she is most definitely naked. All of this is viewed with tolerance by the Council of Ten who rule over Venice, until the forces of moral outrage (usually incensed husbands) rise to the fore, and Casanova is forced to flee.

In the adventures that follow, he comes across alternately as a cheeky opportunist or a kind of Robin Hood figure standing up for the defenceless. One of these is Thérèse, whom he rescues from a potential rape by her aristocratic guardian in a beautifully constructed night-time tavern scene, made up of small glances in close-up, intercut with visually represented sounds as Casanova listens to the struggle through the wall. It is she, in the end, who will rescue Casanova from prison back in Venice and send him into exile for ever. In the impassioned farewell, we think for a moment that he has found a love like none of the others but minutes later, as he boards a ship pursued by guards, he spots another young girl and we know that his adventures have taught him nothing.

Dir: Alexandre Volkoff; **Scr**: Alexandre Volkoff, Ivan Mosjoukine, Norbert Falk; **Ph**: F. Bourgasoff; **Art Dir**: Noë Bloch; **Costume**: Boris Bilinsky; **Cast**: Ivan Mosjoukine, Suzanne Bianchetti, Jenny Jugo.

The Cheat
US, 1915 – 59 mins
Cecil B. DeMille

Looking at *The Cheat* from a twenty-first-century perspective, one could see it as a pared-down 'film noir'. It has all the elements: the subdued lighting, the use of shadow (e.g. the shadows of prison bars on the face of the husband), the twists and turns of fate, sensationalism, sex, suspense and gunshots. But this is, of course, anachronistic. 'Noir' is a category, like Horror, that is used in film studies, and which we now project back onto films that were neither thought of nor conceived of as such by their makers and audiences. Nevertheless, thinking of *The Cheat* as noirish may explain something of its subsequent reputation. The film has an undeniably modern look, the result of good set design and novel use of lighting. It has a modern sensibility with little hint of nineteenth-century morality. If you didn't know, you could easily place this film in the 1920s rather than the teens.

The story concerns Edith, a spoiled young wife and socialite indulged by her stockbroker husband, who struggles to supply her with the clothes and trinkets she needs to keep up with her society friends. She is escorted around town by a sophisticated Japanese ivory trader (Tori), whom we see in the opening shot, marking his possessions with a hot iron. Edith gambles and loses $10,000 raised by the society ladies for the Red Cross, on a stock tip. In desperation, she appeals to Tori for a loan, affording him the opportunity to extort the promise of sexual favours. Her husband gives her the means to repay the loan, but Tori's reaction to her 'cheat' is violent and he claims possession by branding her. Defending her honour, Edith shoots him, but her husband is accused of the crime, leading to the sensational trial in which she bares all to reveal the truth.

Two key scenes linger in the mind which connect with a more modern style of film-making – when Tori is shot by Edith, we see him silhouetted against a paper screen smearing blood as he falls; in the other notorious sequence, enraged with her for trying to buy her way out of their deal, Tori overpowers Edith, branding her flesh with his mark. The struggle is convincingly brutal and realistic, enabling DeMille to depict what is essentially a rape on screen rather than cutting away. It is intended to shock, and it does.

Looking at *The Cheat* more correctly from the nineteenth-century perspective, we can see how much the film owes to stage melodrama, of which DeMille had considerable experience, as did his star technicians, cameraman Alvin Wyckoff and art director Wilfred Buckland. With the exception of Sessue Hayakawa's minimalistic acting, which is a revelation (his exotic/erotic appeal is very reminiscent of later star Rudolph Valentino), the acting, particularly Fannie Ward's, is conventionally gestural in the Griffith style. The scenario adopts the three-act structure of melodrama, which explains why, having reached the emotional climax of the film, we have to labour through several scenes of exposition in the courtroom sequence. Also difficult for the modern audience is the racist reaction of the courtroom mob to the Japanese plaintiff, who has had the presumption to seduce a white woman. In fact, it rankled sufficiently with contemporary audiences for Hayakawa's character to be re-presented as Burmese in the intertitles for the 1918 re-release. Despite some flaws, more noticeable to us than to contemporaries, the film put DeMille on the map and left a significant legacy for European (Abel Gance for one) and classical Hollywood film-makers.

Dir: Cecil B. DeMille; **Scr**: Hector Turnbull, Jeanie McPherson; **Ph**: Alvin Wyckoff; **Art Dir**: Wilfred Buckland; **Cast**: Fannie Ward, Jack Dean, Sessue Hayakawa.

Un Chien andalou
France, 1928 – 16 mins
Luis Buñuel

If *Battleship Potemkin** and *Metropolis** are the most famous of all silent films, then *Un Chien andalou* is arguably the most influential on film as art. Its images have achieved iconic status: the juxtaposition of a cloud crossing the moon with a woman's eye being slashed with a razor is one of the best known in cinema; the hole in a hand, out of which ants are emerging, has become a horror-movie staple; while the androgynous dreamer inexplicably poking a severed hand with a stick, oblivious to the gathering crowd in the street, seems to open up the possibilities of film to communicate at a subconscious level in a way that no other image does.

Inexplicability is the order of the day with *Un Chien andalou*, a 16-minute film conceived by the good friends and fellow Surrealist artists, Luis Buñuel and Salvador Dali. To describe the film is fairly pointless, as it defies any normal narrative logic, but that is the point: as Buñuel himself said of its conception, 'no idea or image that might lend itself to a rational explanation of any kind would be accepted'. The idea, central to the Surrealists' project, was that the viewer should make the meaning. Freud's famous description of the dream as 'the royal road to the unconscious' piqued their interest, and film provided the perfect medium for mapping this road. Unhampered as yet by strictly codified language, the newest art could exploit the extra dimension of time to convey dream logic in a way that painting or literature could not.

The dream logic does explain some aspects of the film, or at least stops the viewer worrying too much about meaning. The first thing to note about *Un Chien andalou* is how different it is from films made by other artists. The film-making style is conventional and plain, with no recourse to abstract or impressionistic/expressionist devices. There are no distortions, no fantastical sets, just a number of characters, objects and locations, some of which have relationships to each other (the moon and the eye, the striped box and the tie, underarm hair and a sea urchin).

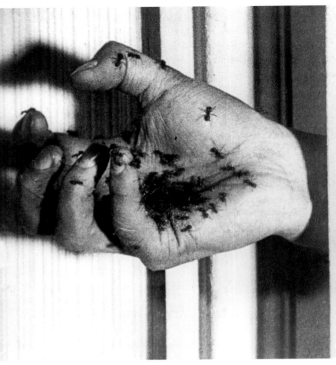

This image of ants crawling out of a human hand is intended to shock

And then there are events – the slicing of the eye; the groping of the woman by the man; the woman stepping outside her apartment onto a beach; the incident of the androgene and the severed hand; the shooting of one of the male characters; and the final shot of the lovers buried up to their necks in sand. Sometimes, the scenes are linked with eyeline matches, sometimes not. There are inserted titles – 'Once upon a time', '8 years later', '16 years earlier', 'Around 3 in the morning' – that don't seem to relate to the picture in any way. These establish a mood of gentle irony which is emphasised by Buñuel's choice of music (played from gramophone records for the premiere and later synchronised) – part of Wagner's *Tristan and Isolde* and a tango. Like a dream, it has that non-threatening air of puzzlement, in which random components are assembled together in a generally chaotic muddle but with recurring elements and a consistent mood. We don't expect it to make sense, so if you find any meaning in this film, it's in your head not mine.

Dir: Luis Buñuel; **Scr**: Luis Buñuel, Salvador Dali; **Ph**: Duverger; **Cast**: Simonne Mareuil, Pierre Batcheff, Luis Buñuel, Jaume Miravitlles, Salvador Dali, Jeanne Rucar.

A Cottage on Dartmoor
UK, 1929 – 87 mins
Anthony Asquith

In a provincial hairdresser's salon, a man is being shaved. He is flirting with the manicurist seated at his side buffing his nails. She responds in an animated fashion, smiling up at him. The camera cuts to the face of the barber, a younger man, whose hands shake as he holds the razor, a picture of repressed jealous rage. The tension winds up as he is forced to watch the couple laugh together, locked in their own secret and exclusive world. Backwards and forwards, faster and faster, the camera cuts from one to the other in tighter and tighter close-up. Then, he sees the engagement ring. As she displays it for effect and the couple touch hands, he reaches breaking point, the razor slashes, a rope snaps, a great gun explodes and the screen lights up blood red: 'Don't move or I'll cut your throat!'

This is the key scene from Anthony Asquith's masterly thriller, *A Cottage on Dartmoor*, which is set in a small-town hairdressing salon and depicts the effects of jealousy on a trio of characters. A young barber, Joe (Uno Henning), who is is trying to court Sally (Norah Baring), the beautiful manicurist, asks her out to see a 'talkie', the latest novelty at the local cinema. She rejects him in favour of the security offered by an older, wealthier farmer. In a jealous rage, Joe slashes the farmer with the razor and is sent to Dartmoor for attempted murder. But he escapes and crosses the moors to find Sally. It is at this point, when she encounters him alone in her remote cottage, not knowing if he means to kill her or ask her forgiveness, that the film begins. The rest of the story is told in flashback.

Of all the British silent films now resurfacing, *A Cottage on Dartmoor* is the most significant rediscovery. The film is a virtuoso work, in which Asquith uses montages of objects, actions and surreal suggestion to express a character's innermost thought. If, stylistically, it recalls German Expressionism and Soviet film-making, it should – Asquith was an avid student of the European cinema – but the film also has its own style. Where Kuleshov, Pudovkin and Eisenstein used such relational editing techniques to portray great events on the world stage, Asquith employs them to serve his more intimate narrative. Not everyone liked it. Oswell Blakeston, in *Close Up*, sneered at the 'thought images' for being too literal, while Rotha accused Asquith of being flashy. But if the technique showed too much – and watching this film can evoke the cold abstraction of the art gallery – it was nevertheless greatly admired for its direction, camerawork and lighting. For the modern audience, its deliberate showiness functions as a fascinating masterclass in late silent film-making technique.

But despite the film being conceived and shot as a silent, sound film had arrived in earnest in early 1930 and the producers felt obliged to release *A Cottage on Dartmoor* as a part-talkie. Confronted by a similar dilemma to the one that Hitchcock faced with *Blackmail* later in that year, Asquith came up with an incredibly neat temporary solution to the technical problem of synchronising the sound without sacrificing the fluidity of the camera movement: in the scene where the cinema audience first encounter the 'talkies', he simply shot their reaction to the sound coming from the screen rather than actually showing it. The soundtrack, which was recorded to disc, doesn't survive, and is one reason why the film was hardly shown after its initial release.

Dir: Anthony Asquith; **Ph**: Stanley Rodwell, Axel Lindblom; **Art Dir**: Ian Campbell-Gray; **Cast**: Uno Henning, Norah Baring, Hans von Schlettow.

Daybreak (Tianming)
China, 1933 – 116 mins
Sun Yu

The West's rediscovery of Chinese silent cinema has been a long time coming but is currently well under way, and at least a handful of classics from the so-called 'golden age' are now accessible on DVD and online. These include the late silents made in Shanghai, China's most culturally international city, during its heyday in the late 1920s and early 30s, before the Japanese invasion put a stop to film production in 1937. The Shanghai studios were well funded and employed film-makers like Sun Yu, who had studied American technique in New York and applied it with great competence to his feature films. The delay in converting to sound allowed the Shanghai studios to produce some incredibly accomplished silent films that exploited all the elegancies of well-honed film grammar without the compromises facing westerners in the early 1930s as they struggled with the new technology.

Daybreak, the second film made by Sun Yu, is a particularly good example of this. As with the late silent films produced in Japan during these years, the storytelling is economical and beautifully executed, every shot has purpose and is held for exactly the right time, the editing is tight and the camera movements very fluid (in one particularly good sequence, as the young couple mount the stairs of a tall tenement building, the camera glides impossibly through the fabric of the building). With few artistic shots and little montage, the films of Sun Yu and his contemporaries have much in common with the classic Hollywood tradition of the 1930s and 40s rather than the silent period and, as such, are very articulate and accessible.

Many Chinese silents of this period foreground women protagonists, typically as the victims of men and circumstances, and are tragic in tone. *Daybreak* is a variation on this theme. The heroine, Ling Ling, is a simple country girl who, like hundreds of others, flees the countryside for the city to escape the punitive warlord regime. In the big city, she and her fiancé and childhood sweetheart, Zhang, fall foul of the oppressive factory-owners and are separated; Ling Ling is raped by her employer's son and forced to wander the streets, where she is trapped by an apparently kindly old man and sold to a brothel. The difference between this film and others in the same tragic mode is that Ling Ling vows to free herself and others from oppression and becomes fired with revolutionary zeal; escaping from the brothel when the Nationalists invade the city, she turns herself into a kind of Mati Hari, exploiting men (which she learns to do very well) to help her poor neighbours.

When reunited with Zhang, now a revolutionary activist being pursued by warlord soldiers, she uses all her powers of seduction to distract them while he gets away – in one surprising close-up, her stockinged leg fills the screen like the famous shot from *The Graduate* (1967). The sequence is as tense as any film noir, and Ling Ling is as feisty as any noir heroine when the game is up. What remain with you, though, are the flashback scenes (in sharp contrast to the dark of the city), where she recalls her youth, floating among the water-chestnut ponds with Zhang in a bright sunlit idyll of love, innocence and underlying sensuality. She returns to this innocent state as, dressed again in her country clothes, she faces her final dawn.

Dir/**Scr**: Sun Yu; **Ph**: Zhou Ke; **Cast**: Li Lili, Gao Zhanfei, Ye Juanjuan, Yuan Congmei.

Les Deux Timides (Two Timid Souls)
France, 1928 – 76 mins
Réne Clair

I'm going to be in trouble for not selecting *The Italian Straw Hat* (*Un Chapeau de paille d'italie*, 1928) as my second René Clair film, which is a superior film in some ways, but I have a good reason, and that is to briefly explore how the really technically proficient directors of the late 1920s approached the coming of sound and if it affected their late silent works. Not unlike today's anxiety about the death of celluloid, the prospect of the coming of the talkies was unsettling. The silent cinema had by the late 1920s developed a level of sophistication that was under threat by the new technology, but, like the digital revolution, the coming of sound could not be ignored. There is evidence in the work of several directors that they are thinking about how to incorporate sound. Hitchcock, for example, uses images of sounds over edits as early as *The Ring* (1927) (a kettle boils over, the sudden shriek interrupting an illicit meeting), a technical flourish that he would use to great effect in his sound films. Ozu, in *I Was Born, But …**, straightforwardly represents a verbal argument as if to demonstrate he could just drop the dialogue into his film anytime, while Asquith ducked the issue in *A Cottage on Dartmoor** by divorcing the image from the talking so that he could retain his virtuoso camera and editing style.

In *Les Deux Timides*, Clair does something a bit different, and very clever, which is to produce a scene that could *only* be accomplished in a silent film. It's a gimmick but it's brilliant. Like *The Italian Straw Hat* the film is a classic imbroglio farce, by Eugene Labiche and Marc Michel, concerning a father who is too timid to prevent a wife-beating bully from courting his daughter and a young attorney too timid to ask the father for the daughter's hand.

In the opening scene, the young attorney, Frémissin, played with great skill by Pierre Batcheff, is making his first trial speech, defending the obviously guilty wife-beater Garadoux. The prosecution have just outlined the case against, which is represented in a stylised vignette showing the villain in a squalid room hitting his oppressed seamstress wife and stealing her money. As Frémissin gets to his feet and makes his case, the image dissolves to a contrasting vignette in which the room, now bright and airy, is occupied by the dutiful wife sitting at her leisure stitching something lacy as she awaits the homecoming of the loving husband bearing flowers. As Frémissin lays it on with a trowel, accompanied by appropriately grandiloquent gestures, the audience is clearly enjoying this moving scene (represented in increasingly subdivided split-screen scenes to pile on the examples of the husband's devotion to his wife). The judges, meanwhile, have presumably heard it all before and are yawning wearily when suddenly a mouse runs out. In the ensuing mêlée, Frémissin loses his thread and when asked to resume becomes flustered. He repeats his story, and so we dissolve again to Garadoux as he enters the room and greets his wife, but this time they suddenly freeze in mid-action as Frémissin goes blank. He resumes, the audience beginning to fidget, and Garadoux comes in once again and freezes once more. As Frémissin fumbles with his notes, then, eyes closed, tries to mentally retrace his steps, the scene in the room is literally played in reverse as Garadoux walks backwards out of the door. A whirling spiral fills the screen as, hopelessly confused, Frémissin calls for the maximum penalty to be imposed on the client he is supposed to be defending.

Clair, having perhaps proved his point about the superiority of silent film, then went on to make some of the best early sound films, including *Sous les toits de Paris* (1930) and *Le Million* (1931).

Dir/Scr: René Clair; **Ph**: Robert Batton, Nikolas Roudakoff; **Cast**: Pierre Batcheff, Jim Gérald, Vera Flory, M. M. Maurice de Féraudy.

Douro, faina fluvial (Labour on the Douro River)
Portugal, 1931 – 21 mins
Manoel de Oliveira

At the time of writing, I have just booked to see the latest film by
Manoel de Oliveira, *The Strange Case of Angelica* (2010), which is set in
his birthplace, Porto, just like his first film, *Douro, faina fluvial*. At 101
going on 102, he is the only living director to have made a film in the
silent era. The new film, I am told, is not only experimental, taking as its
subject a dead girl who lives only through a young photographer's
camera lens, but also has a few nods to the silent days. It is clear from
watching *Douro faina fluvial* that it is the experimental that interests him.
A homage to *Berlin, Symphony of a City**, which Oliveira is on record as
saying had a direct influence on him, the film does indeed use many of
the same film-making techniques – unusual angles, rhythmic editing, an
observational style, ordinary objects seen in new ways.

Its subject is the great river of Portugal, the Douro, from the
pounding breakers of the Atlantic coast to the calm waters upstream and
the ordinary people going about their work on the riverbanks. Like the
city symphonies, it is structured around the day, starting with the lights
of the lighthouse and proceeding through the bustle of the morning's
work – loading and unloading, selling in the marketplace – moving on to
lunchtime when the people and their animals stop to eat, followed by
the calm of the siesta in the afternoon heat. Here we see the town, its
buildings, washing-strewn alleyways, tiled roofscapes, train sidings.
As the afternoon wears on, the work becomes more frenetic, with traffic,
ox carts and cars competing in the narrow streets. An accident injects a
short narrative, as a plane distracts a driver and a frenzied ox bolts,
trampling on a young man. A girl screams in alarm, but he is not hurt
and dashes off to calm the beast.

There is perhaps more of a painterly eye than we find in Ruttmann's
Berlin …, as Oliveira and cameraman Antonio Mendes use blurring of
focus to bring out the play of light on water or the impression of

starlight from the lighthouse lamps. Oliveira's remarkably confident editing establishes relationships between objects in rapid juxtapositions – arrangements of wood in alignment with heaps of glimmering fish on the quayside – that comment on their qualities as abstract images. Lines created by the boats' rigging wobbling in watery reflections, the tight diagonal line of an anchor chain pulling against the tide or the struts of the great iron bridge from a worm's-eye view all build to an impressionistic culmination as the day ends and the lighthouse starts its night-time vigil once more.

Dir: Manoel de Oliveira; **Ph**: Antonio Mendes.

Drifters
UK, 1929 – 49 mins
John Grierson

It is difficult to separate John Grierson's *Drifters* from its place in cinema history, for it was at once the herald of a different model of film-making with progressive social purpose and his homage to Eisenstein and the European avant-garde. The film was not so much the expression of an artistic voice but was made with a definite purpose dreamed up by the head of the Empire Marketing Board, Stephen Tallents, to persuade the British government of the benefits of financing film as part of his brief to rebrand the Empire. Even the subject matter, the threatened herring industry, was chosen advisedly, for the financial secretary to the Treasury had written a work of economic history on the subject and it was this that probably secured the funding for the pilot project. Besides, the lives of the trawlermen had a romance about them that was already a favourite with film-makers, and Grierson had a good deal of experience of the sea, having served on minesweepers during the war.

There is a long tradition of trawler films that stretches from the earliest days of film to the present, in TV series such as the BBC's *Trawlermen* or Hollywood films like *The Perfect Storm* (2000). The early films established a pattern and mood for portraying this dangerous and vital profession, which has been copied and passed down remarkably intact over more than a century. *Drifters* is no exception to the blueprint – from Mitchell & Kenyon's films in 1901 to *Trip to the North Sea Fisheries* in 1909 and *Heroes of the North Sea* (1925), they all follow the logic of the 'trip', from leaving the harbour, setting the nets, hauling in the fish, processing the catch and returning home. They nearly all show scenes of rough seas, the nonchalant bravery of the crew and their joyful spirit as they play games on the home run, as well as their competence with the mechanics of the trawler. They all finish with the bringing of the fish to market, emphasising the contrast between the effort and danger undergone by the crew and the cheapness and banality of the commodity – the humble herring which is taken for granted by the customer. It is this powerful emotive statement that all of these films have in common.

Where *Drifters* differs from the tradition of the trawler films is stylistically. Grierson was a great admirer of the European avant-garde and his clearest influence is Eisenstein, but the adoption of the montage editing or the detached, observational style so reminiscent of *Rien que les heures* (1926) or *Berlin, Symphony of a City** is not entirely slavish. The rapid cutting seems peculiarly appropriate to the choppy seas and thundering machinery. Grierson also tempered the Russian style, underplaying the heroics and avoiding close-ups or gleaming musculature; there is nothing self-consciously arty in the European mode; this is very much 'documentary' – in his own famous phrase, the 'creative treatment of reality'. The ambitious Grierson had the bare-faced cheek to inveigle his film into the prestigious programme of the Film Society which premiered *Battleship Potemkin**, where he sat in nervous silence with Stephen Tallents – it was received 'rapturously'. However compromised *Drifters* might be in terms of its original mission – it is not entirely successful, with a clunky underwater sequence – it was good enough for that refined audience and in the end it is a beautiful film.

Dir: John Grierson; **Ph**: Basil Emmott.

Earth (*Zemlya*)
USSR, 1930 – 78 mins
Aleksandr Dovzhenko

Soviet Russia in 1929/30 wasn't an auspicious time or place to be a
Ukrainian nationalist trying to make films about Ukrainian culture.
When Aleksandr Dovzhenko took on the assignment to make a picture
about Stalin's new collectivisation scheme, it seemed innocuous enough,
but by the time *Earth* was released in 1930 it had already become
evident, particularly in the Ukraine, that the policy to mechanise
agriculture in order to force the pace of industrialisation in the cities was
a disaster. As a consequence, the film was not especially well received
but it is now seen as Dovzhenko's masterpiece, a film of lyrical beauty
and aesthetic originality that anticipates the style of Tarkovsky and
Parajanov. While Dovzhenko retained the rapid editing and montage
technique of his fellow Russian film-makers, he also had the eye of the
graphic artist – the big skies of the Ukrainian landscape are beautifully
composed, bisected by a single line of telegraph poles or the crisp edges
of a stand of wheat, and he uses a lot of close-ups of ripe apples on the
trees and the faces of the peasants. There are almost no establishing
shots to provide a spatial or temporal point of reference; we see only
what the director wants us to see.

   The opening shot of the wind blowing the wheat in the deserted
fields cuts to a girl standing next to a huge sunflower in bright light
against an empty sky, followed by a close-up of apples on a branch and
an old man lying under the trees. Other people appear – a young
woman, babies playing among the fallen apples, another old man,
a friend – but we never establish their relationship to one another.
The friend asks the old man if he is dying, and it seems he is, but first he
talks for a while and eats a pear before crossing his hands and lying
down to die. It is remarked that for seventy-five years he ploughed the
fields with oxen – a heroic feat under such a punishing workload. But it
is a good death, and one that few of us could hope for – certainly not

The pastoral idyll of an orchard as counterpoint for the terrible events that follow

Dovzhenko, whose wish to die on his native soil was denied by the Soviet authorities, and not for the millions of Russian agricultural workers who would die miserably as a result of collectivisation.

The death of the old man in the orchard surrounded by bounty and babies playing establishes the film's themes of birth, death and rebirth. It is almost religious in tone, the orchard representing a little heaven populated by cherubs. But there is a serpent in paradise. The matter of collectivisation centres on a feud between the richer kulaks, who would defend their property to the death, and the poorer family whose son

Vasili leads the younger generation, the komsomols, towards the new way (they have combined to bring in a tractor that will save the manual labour which is crushing the people). The Fordson tractor is almost fetishised as it completes the work of hundreds with speedy efficiency. But Vasili has ploughed up the kulaks' fences, leading inevitably to violence, during which he is shot by the resentful kulak's son. Grief-stricken, Vasili's father takes up the cause of the collective, burying his son in the new way, with no priests or God. The funeral becomes the focus for the community's decision to collectivise, their singing drowning out the ravings of Vasili's killer and the now powerless and irrelevant priest. As the corpse of her elder son is carried along under the apple trees, Vasili's mother gives birth, and thus the continuity of life is maintained.

Dir/Scr: Aleksandr Dovzhenko; **Ph**: Daniil Demutsky; **Cast**: Stepan Shkurat, Semyon Svashenko, Yuliya Solntseva.

En dirigeable sur les champs de bataille
France, 1918 – 78 mins
Lucien Le Sainte

Given that the sum of all silent film is finite, it may seem strange that new discoveries are being made all the time. Films sit in the vaults either unpreserved, and therefore unknown by the world outside, or just waiting for their moment to emerge into the light, impelled by some new piece of research, an archivist's curiosity, a festival programmer's passion, the arrival of new technologies to make them available or the insatiable appetites of television producers for what they call 'archive' or 'content'. But however much the archivists may harrumph at television presenters who claim to have 'unearthed' their great 'discoveries' by 'delving in the vaults', when all they have done is look in the catalogue or on the perfectly clean, well-organised shelves, the recent interest in actuality archive film of all kinds can only be a good thing. Since the release in 2005 of the Mitchell & Kenyon films (see *Alfred Butterworth & Sons* …*), television has brought many more of these fabulous early collections to light, the most stunning being the Albert Kahn collection in France, a concerted effort by a rich philanthropist to document an increasingly globalised world in his 'Archive of the Planet'. This combines 72,000 autochrome colour photographs with the films. The very high-resolution images somehow remove the barrier between us and the people of the last century, while the films supply the overview.

One of these films, *En dirigeable sur les champs de bataille*, exhibited at a festival a few years ago, and recently screened in extract on BBC 2, surprised me utterly, because it presented a completely different view of something I thought I knew well. Now held by ECPAD, the French military archives, but apparently sponsored by the Albert Kahn project, the film was taken simply to document the devastation along the Western Front shortly after the armistice in December 1918. Lucien Le Sainte, an experienced Gaumont cameraman now working for Kahn, was piloted by French naval officer Jacques Trolley de Prévaux in a navy airship along the front from Nieuport on the coast of Belgium to Reims in the Champagne region of France.

It is an extraordinary experience to see miles and miles of zigzag trenches from the air as we drift slowly (rather than zooming hysterically over it in a plane) at an altitude low enough for the pilot to wave at the few individuals who have crept back to seek out their homes in the ruins, and low enough to shave the top of the ruined stump of the cathedral at Armentières. This silent drifting suits perfectly the mood of contemplation that characterised the immediate aftermath of war – the constant barrage was finally over, the dust had settled and it was time to see what was left. From up here, the answer is not much – piles of stones, scorched wooden beams that once held up houses and medieval abbeys, the odd spike of a cathedral tower, the carcasses of tanks and the pattern of roads now the only clue to the location of the towns and villages that once stood there. As we float across no-man's-land, the water-filled pockmarks in the mud look at first like puddles until you notice in the distance a bridge or part of a ruined building that defines the scale of this vast landscape of craters. There is no comment from the film-makers, only a title now and then to give you a rough location. Words are no good here – our only duty is to look and reflect.

Dir/Ph: Lucien Le Sainte; **Pilot**: Jacques Trolley de Prévaux.

The Fall of the House of Usher (La Chute de la maison Usher)
France, 1928 – 63 mins
Jean Epstein

Jean Epstein's *Fall of the House of Usher* is no easier to understand at first than the Edgar Allan Poe story (of 1839) but, like the story, it is really worth persisting. The film is short, just 63 minutes, and the plot fairly simple: a stranger (the unnamed narrator) is summoned by a friend's letter to the grim castle of Usher, where he finds his friend Roderick Usher suffering from nervous debility and his wife, Madeline, dying of a mysterious illness. Roderick is painting a supernaturally lifelike portrait of Madeline paying ferocious attention to it while the life force of its human subject ebbs away, unnoticed. She dies and is interred in a vault, but during a massive electrical storm she reappears, as a hysterical Roderick divulges that she has been buried alive. The storm destroys the mansion as the three flee from the scene.

Epstein's story is in fact a composite of two Poe stories, 'The Fall of the House of Usher' and 'The Oval Portrait', as the opening credits explain: 'd'après les motifs de Edgar A. Poe'. In fact, everything about the film is quite precise, despite what you might read in the host of very badly researched reviews on the web. While the film is not a faithful rendition of the title story, it is a serious attempt to capture the layers and complexity of Poe's writings. Epstein had immersed himself in Poe, not just the gothic stories but also his essays on spatial and temporal relationships, even down to the décor and furniture which inform the set design of the film (the massive hall of the House of Usher is a kind of precursor of the hall at Xanadu in *Citizen Kane* [1941]). He also drops in witty visual references to two other Poe stories, 'Ligea' and 'The Pit and the Pendulum'. Other changes are more practical – making Roderick and Madeline husband and wife, rather than twin brother and sister, sidesteps any implication of incest and allows him to drop the story of 'The Oval Portrait' into the 'Usher' framework, making an interesting, almost proto-feminist, observation on the husband's neglect of his wife in favour of his manufactured *idea* of her. He also eschews Poe's ending, in which Madeline, back from the grave, falls on her brother killing him, in a very literal 'fall' of both the bloodline of the 'house' of Usher and the physical house, which collapses spectacularly on their death. This is less easy to understand, as the former would surely be more dramatic, but may represent the inclusion of the 'Ligea' plot as the painting burns, releasing the anima of the dead wife.

It is in the building of atmosphere, however, that Epstein hopes to convey the genius of Poe. Using all of his considerable talents as a film-maker, and with the cinematic specificity he always sought, he combines Expressionist settings and lighting with the Impressionist techniques for which he was better known: slow motion, mobile lighting effects, high and low camera angles, and the superimpositions (including the use of negative images to express the departure of Madeline's soul from her body) for which the film is often noted. The sense of isolation, redundancy and dread of the Usher's asocial world is well observed, as are its grisly surroundings full of miasmas, copulating toads and fungal protuberances. Time drags and speeds up, a cold wind is always blowing through the vast spaces of the house. Epstein makes visual Poe's own thoughts on story composition, in which environment is critical: 'a close circumscription of space is absolutely necessary to the effect of insulated incident – it has the force of a frame to a picture. It has an indisputable moral power in keeping concentrated the attention, and, of course, must not be confounded with mere unity of place.'[9]

Dir: Jean Epstein: **Ph**: Georges Lucas/Jean Lucas; **Art Dir**: Pierre Kéfer; **Cast**: Jean Debucourt, Charles Lamy, Marguerite Gance, Fournez-Goffard.

Finis terrae
France, 1929 – 88 mins
Jean Epstein

The opening title of Jean Epstein's *Finis terrae* nails its colours to the mast – 'This is not a fiction – it is a reconstitution of a drama inspired by the particular conditions in a certain little known area of our country. The actors in this film are the very people who are the players in real life.' It marks a point somewhere on the sliding scale between drama and documentary where we also find *Nanook of the North*, The Great White Silence** and *Battleship Potemkin*,* among others. It is a true story, filmed on location. The players are not professional actors and belong to the specific place. And yet, all of these films have different proportions of truth and fiction, intervention and intention.

Epstein is mostly associated with his avant-garde fiction films, so the series of pictures he made in Brittany, starting with *Finis terrae* in 1929, seems like a radical departure. In fact, he carries over some of his film-making techniques from earlier works but at the same time chooses quite specifically to use local people to act out this story (almost too strong a word) even though they were not the actual individuals concerned. He attributes a collective spirit to the people of the region, and this comes out strongly in the narrative when the community of Ouessant (Ushant) become anxious about the welfare of the men and boys who are isolated on the barren islet of Bannec for the summer, burning seaweed for soda to sell to the factories. The local doctor, a popular leader of the community (with a hint of the saintly), goes to their aid across the treacherous tidal seas that divide the Breton isles from the mainland.

As with other films in the drama-documentary spectrum, the beauty of the landscape and the objects in it is a major and exquisite feature. The local people form part of this authentic scenery – their faces, their clothes, their houses and boats are all quite distinctive, while the texture of rocks, flowers and sand are almost fetishised. Small objects

Non-professional, local actors lend realism to a Breton tale near Ouessant

(emphasised through the use of close-up) like a bottle, a knife or a loaf
of bread take on significance, as if objects in a Flemish still life.
The lighthouse, with its ribbed fresnel lens, is a recurring image, a symbol
of home, strength and stability. When one of the boys becomes delirious
with blood poisoning, it is the lighthouse that begins to rock and sway,
suggestive of his dangerously ill state.

　　Epstein's techniques draw on Impressionism and the range of
avant-garde devices that you find in his previous films, such as *Fall of the
House of Usher** – rapid cutting, distortions, tracking shots, extreme

angles, and so on. Where he used speeded-up film in the funeral sequence of *Usher*, in *Finis terrae* he employs the opposite: by over-cranking, he imparts subtle touches of slow motion to a person's face in a reaction shot or to point up a mannerism indicative of their state of mind; and, in my particular favourite, he applies the same technique to images of the crashing waves as they thunder down on the rocky coast, so that they rise up and pause for a fraction of a second – it's the nearest thing to music I know of in silent film.

Dir: Jean Epstein; **Ph**: Joseph Barthès, Joseph Kottula, with Louis Née, R. Tulle; **Cast**: Gibois, Jean-Marie Laot, Malgorn, François Morin, Pierre, Ambroise Rouzic.

Flesh and the Devil
US, 1926 – 112 mins
Clarence Brown

There is 'It' (see *It**) and there is chemistry, which is basically 'It' times
two. Chemistry is one of the most bankable assets of the Hollywood star
system but like 'It' is difficult to define and harder to find. MGM were
lucky that a relatively random pairing brought together two 'A' list stars
who suddenly bonded – on screen. But the studio nearly missed the
chance, as they had worked the young Swedish actress to the point of
nervous exhaustion on a film about a beautiful woman who destroys
everyone she comes into contact with, called *The Temptress* (1926).
They refused to let her go home to Sweden to mourn her sister and
pressured her into another film about a beautiful woman who destroys
everyone she comes into contact with, called *Flesh and the Devil*.
John Gilbert was the big star with his name in big above the title, below
which came Greta Garbo and fellow Swede, Lars Hanson. The film was a
conventional romantic tragedy but with a good pedigree, based on a
play by Herman Sudermann, who also wrote the play from which
Sunrise* was adapted. Added to this was another great pairing of
director Clarence Brown and cameraman William Daniels. These two
were responsible for getting the photochemistry to register the sexual
chemistry that exuded from Gilbert and Garbo when they came together
on screen. An instant rapport developed into a passionate love affair
both on and off the set, to the evident delight of audiences when the
film was released.

There are several key scenes in which this chemistry is on full
display. The first is a dance sequence where Leo (Gilbert), already
smitten by Felicitas (Garbo) following a brief meeting, sees her again
and, dropping his partner, asks her to dance. Looking from side to side,
she excuses herself to her companions, drawing attention to one
beautiful shoulder after another; then, in one extraordinary movement,
she looks directly into his eyes, raises her face almost to his lips and,

taking him by the shoulder, pulls him into the waltz. A contrasting shot of his abandoned partner, a young girl who is asked to dance by a much younger and much shorter boy, makes the point that there is dancing – and dancing. Back the camera goes in a tight two-shot from above as they twist and turn, nearly but not quite mouth to mouth. The scene extends into the garden, where they sit in a secluded arbour. A lit match illumines their faces as they devour each other with their eyes, till she blows it softly out.

From this point on, it is clear that their passion will mow down everything in its path. As they lie in post-coital euphoria, beautifully composed, kissing on a chaise longue, the husband arrives home and a duel ensues. Gilbert kills his man and is sent off by the army to Africa as punishment. He asks his childhood friend Ulrich (Lars Hanson) to look after Felicitas. After three years, he returns to find Ulrich married to her and tries to stay away, but fate intervenes and an ailing Ulrich summons his friend. The passion between the two inevitably resumes but despite being unable to resist, Leo feels increasingly manipulated and eventually rebels, with tragic consequences. The ending is a bit trite, which was commented on at the time, but nobody cared. They had seen the real thing on screen – chemistry – the formula for which eludes studio executives to this day.

Dir: Clarence Brown; **Ph**: William Daniels; **Scr**: Benjamin Glazer, from the play by Hermann Sudermann; **Cast**: John Gilbert, Greta Garbo, Lars Hanson, Marc McDermott.

The General
US, 1926 – 76 mins
Clyde Bruckman, Buster Keaton

It would be easier, in a way, for the purposes of this book to write about
two other Buster Keaton features, *The Cameraman* (1928) or *Sherlock Jr*
(1924). Both have that reflexivity about the nature of the cinema that is
interesting to explore, but this would mean missing out on one of silent
cinema's greatest joys and a frequent denizen of the top ten greatest
films of all time, *The General*. This perfectly judged film is not reflexive at
all and manages to pull off the difficult transition from comedy to the
feature film form by organising itself around a situation rather than a
series of gags. The best gags in the film all arise out of the central
premise, loosely based on a Civil War story, of a railway line that has
Union troops at one end and the Confederates at the other.

The engineer, Johnny, our hero, is a Southerner and is in love with his
engine, 'The General', and his gal, Annabelle. When the war comes to
town, Annabelle's brother and father enlist immediately and Johnny is
first in line at the recruiting office but is turned down because the officer
thinks he is more useful on the footplate than in the infantry; crucially,
however, he doesn't tell him this. Annabelle, suspecting Johnny of
malingering, refuses to speak to him until he is in uniform. So our hero
must overcome this unjust state of affairs, and when 'The General' is
hijacked by Northern agents, and Annabelle with it, he must pursue
them to win the girl and the war.

The railway and the train give scope to Keaton's genius with
mechanical devices and produce some of the best gags of his career.
In one sequence, he sits in a melancholy reverie on the connecting rod
between the engine's wheels, his motionless body lifting up and down in
a reflection of his sigh as the train begins to move. And then there is the
sublime episode with the canon which has been mounted on the back of
his train: disappointed by the damp squib of the first shot powered by an
elegant pinch of gunpowder, Johnny recklessly tips the entire contents

into the barrel and then contrives to get his foot caught in the coupling, thus lowering the canon's trajectory till it is pointing straight at him not the enemy. In everyone's favourite moment, Johnny picks up one railway sleeper, intended to derail him, off the tracks when another hoves into view – with a child's logic, he uses it like jackstraws to catapult the other out of the train's path just in time.

Buster Keaton's impeccable logic gets him out of a tricky situation and demonstrates how to play spillikins with a train and a railway sleeper

Keaton's profound, often underestimated, understanding of the audience (who hasn't played jackstraws) allows him to create a feeling of verisimilitude that lifts *The General* onto a higher plain. It is a good story full of great gags and real romance (the scene in the engine cab where Annabelle is ineffectually throwing tiny bits of wood into the firebox as the enemy are upon them and an exasperated Johnny goes to wring her neck, then kisses her instead, is one of the most charming moments in cinema history). It is a perfectly balanced narrative trajectory but best of all is the persona and person of Buster Keaton.

Dir: Clyde Bruckman, Buster Keaton; **Ph**: Dev Jennings, Bert Haines; **Cast**: Buster Keaton, Marion Mack, Glen Cavender.

The Gold Rush
US, 1925 – 96 mins (at 24fps)
Charles Chaplin

The Gold Rush is the film Chaplin said he would most like to be
remembered for, and it's easy to see why. Chaplin was at his peak in
1923, having gained experience of the feature-film form with *The Kid**
and *A Woman of Paris* (1923). The latter was a sophisticated adult
drama, in which Chaplin did not himself appear but which clearly
demonstrated his ability to craft longer films. The public were not
apparently ready for a Chaplin film without the Little Tramp and the film
did poorly, so he returned to safer ground with the Little Fellow going off
to the Klondike as the 'lone prospector'. That same year, Buster Keaton
and Harold Lloyd had produced the spectacular comedy features *Our
Hospitality* (1923) and *Safety Last!**, so there may also have been an
element of competition in Chaplin's choice of project.

The pathos, for which he would be alternately loved and hated,
was inherent in the story of physical hardship and privation, but few of
his contemporaries could have extracted such sublime comedy from
starvation and cannibalism. In two of his most magnificent set pieces,
Chaplin draws on English pantomime traditions to effect
transformations. The first is the famous boot scene, in which, trapped in
a cabin with Big Jim, another prospector, in a driving blizzard with no
food, Charlie cooks his own boot. In imitation of a refined Thanksgiving
dinner, he presents the upper, better part to Big Jim and takes the sole
for himself, eating the laces like spaghetti and sucking the hobnails as if
they were chicken bones. In the second sequence, the cabin, blown from
its moorings by the blizzard, is left teetering on the edge of a cliff;
Charlie blames the rocking of the cabin on his hangover and is only
made aware of the emergency when he tries to go outside and finds
himself hanging over empty space. He and Big Jim struggle to keep the
cabin on an even keel and have to climb up the floor to get out. Big Jim
makes it out and finds the prospecting claim he has been seeking,

forgetting all about Charlie, remembering him just in time to throw him a rope as the cabin goes over the edge.

Aside from the set pieces, there is a genuinely touching romance in the film as the lone prospector falls in love with the glamorous dance-hall belle, Georgia, having been led to believe that she returns his affections. He invites her and her friends to a New Year's Eve supper, shovelling snow all day to make enough money for presents and food. When they don't show, he falls asleep and dreams of the good time they would have been having as he entertains the girls with the legendary 'dance of the rolls', in which he makes two rolls on forks dance like a chorus girl. This party piece was not original but the execution of it is perfect and it has rightly become one of the most recognised scenes in cinema history. Donald McCaffrey, in his 1971 collection of critical essays on Chaplin, remarks on his supreme skill as 'a clown who could exhibit the slapstick of Harlequin with the moonstruck sadness of Pierrot … the comedian was able to make us laugh and still feel sorry for this pathetic little man'.[10] This pathos would emerge in a darker manifestation in *City Lights* (1931) and *The Circus* (1928); here it has a lightness of touch that allows the uncharacteristic happy ending to work. Chaplin reissued the film in 1942 with music and his own commentary to cover the intertitles, but the silent version is more elegantly structured.

Dir/Scr: Charles Chaplin; **Ph**: Roland Totheroh; **Cast**: Charles Chaplin, Georgia Hale, Mack Swain, Tom Murray, Malcolm Waite.

Der Golem, wie er in die Welt kam (The Golem: How He Came into the World)
Germany, 1920 – 85 mins
Paul Wegener, Carl Boese

Like *Nosferatu**, *The Golem* has considerable popular appeal outside the rarefied field of silent cinema. If you want to pique the interest of an audience unlikely to be sympathetic to early film, then show them one of these two films. With its story of the creation of a slave creature made from clay that ultimately turns against its magician master, the film works well as a monster movie and, who knows, maybe horror fans will catch some of the allure of silent film while they are watching. *The Golem* also belongs to another genre – Expressionism. The look of the film is what you notice first, from the opening shot of bulging, leaning medieval towers silhouetted against a star-filled astronomer's sky. We are in the realm of fairy tale, magic and necromancy and more or less in sixteenth-century Prague in the Jewish ghetto.

Rabbi Loew foresees disaster for his people in the stars and conjures the demon Astaroth to give him the word that will bring the golem to life. At first, he uses the creature to save the Jews from the Emperor, who wishes to banish them from his lands, but the alignment of the planets also dictates that the golem will turn against his master. Reanimated and used in a jealous rage by Loew's assistant to pursue the knight Florian, who has deflowered the Rabbi's flirtatious daughter Miriam, the golem becomes destroyer not servant, throwing the knight from the top of a tower and dragging Miriam through the streets having set the town on fire. Once more, Rabbi Loew must save the people by extinguishing the fire, and the golem is brought down by a small child who removes the magic word that animates him. It is this scene, in which the monster discovers the innocent charms of the child, that links it with the classics of the horror genre through a similar episode in *Frankenstein* (1931). Paul Wegener's creature originated not only the stiff-legged monster walk but also first evoked the pathos of the monster as child, which becomes

one of the defining features of horror and science fiction. We shouldn't labour this point, however, as Wegener, who co-wrote and directed as well as starred in the film, was primarily interested not so much in the psychological aspects of the story but in the mystical, and had made several films before on a similar theme, including the über-creepy *The Student of Prague** in 1913. Wegener sourced numerous materials for his golem legend (not the book by Meyrink, as is commonly assumed), including Arthur Holitscher's play of 1908, possibly a much earlier tale recorded by Jakob Grimm, Goethe's 'Sorcerer's Apprentice' or Chayim Bloch's *Der Praguer Golem*, among many others. Going back further, the golem derives from the Jewish word meaning 'unformed'.

This manipulation of the 'unformed' is the pervasive image of the film. Unlike the flat sets of *The Cabinet of Dr. Caligari**, *The Golem*'s sets are built – they *are* Expressionist architecture, and were designed by Hans Poelzig. An architect from a generation familiar with the many ephemeral exhibition buildings of that age, Poelzig visually connects the rough clay figure of the golem with the buildings, moulded from the same clay, which lean and bend in a kind of synthesis of fellow architect Gaudi's parabolic curves and the twisting, organic alleys of the medieval town. Gaudi's description of Expressionist or gothic architecture perfectly captures the essence of Expressionist film design:

> Gothic art is imperfect, it means to solve; it is the style of the compass, the formula of industrial repetition. Its stability is based on the permanent propping of abutments: it is a defective body that holds with support ... gothic works produce maximum emotion when they are mutilated, covered with ivy and illuminated by the moon.[11]

Dir: Paul Wegener, Carl Boese; **Scr**: Henrik Galeen, Paul Wegener; **Ph**: Karl Freund; **Cast**: Paul Wegener, Albert Steinrück, Ernst Deutsch, Lyda Salmonova, Lothar Müthel.

(*Opposite page*) A crowd scene in the Jewish ghetto set shows the impressive scope of Expressionist design

Gösta Berlings Saga
Sweden, 1924 – 163 mins
Mauritz Stiller

Some stories lend themselves well to a 3-hour running time and the episodic saga is perfect for it. The word saga might imply stodginess but in fact the time speeds by in Mauritz Stiller's final great work of the first 'golden age' of Swedish cinema, *Gösta Berlings Saga*. In Britain, it was called *The Atonement of Gösta Berling* in an attempt to explain the central thrust of a sometimes confusing plot. The film is based on a celebrated novel of 1891 by Selma Lagerlöf, the first woman to win the Nobel Prize for literature, whose speciality was nineteenth-century Swedish society. The novel has a host of loosely connected characters and subplots, which come together in the denouement.

The story centres on a young defrocked priest called Gösta Berling, played by Lars Hanson, who, having been cast out of his parish for drunkenness, wanders the land in search of some meaning to his life, during the course of which three women fall in love with him, with devastating consequences. The last of these, and the instrument of Gösta's redemption, is played by the as yet unknown Greta Garbo, coached Svengali-like by Stiller for the role, and even though she hadn't developed the style that would make her a huge star in America, the legendary radiance is clear to see. Julius Jaenzon's photography of Lars Hanson and Greta Garbo is exemplary, and also extends to the interiors – for example, the great house at Ekeby is shot with its ceilings in view, an innovation that wouldn't be repeated till *Citizen Kane* in 1941. The most spectacular set piece, however, is the pursuit by wolves of the lovers in their horse-drawn sleigh across a vast frozen lake. Stiller builds the tension by focusing on the trivial conversation between the pair, who are unaware of the wolves we have spotted in the distance. The camera pulls out to reveal the pack almost upon them, then shows them savagely ripping apart a fur thrown from the sleigh. This is clearly not a special effect but quite real and genuinely terrifying.

Greta Garbo and Lars Hanson escape from the wolves

In attempting to synthesise the rich content of the novel, the film becomes slightly disjointed. It could be a consequence of missing material – it was cut down and re-edited several times – but most of the full running length has been recovered. Another explanation could be that the author retained some approval of the script and perhaps was unable to give up certain scenes or characters. There are certainly plenty of them, although the absolute standout is the character of the Mayor's wife, played by Gerda Lundequist, an independent, spirited woman and a natural leader of men, who would not be out of place in an Arthurian legend or a great Western epic. It is she who finally draws together the hero and heroine, breaking their cycle of despair and moral crisis.

Lagerlöf complained about the film, accusing Stiller of watching too many bad serials, but it is precisely the pleasures of the film serial that lift *Gösta Berlings Saga* out of the ordinary – the great spectacles, the sense of immersion in story and character that the long running time bestows. This kind of long, spectacular adventure with exotic locations and romantic characters would become hugely popular in the next few years, and would produce some of silent cinema's highest achievements.

Dir: Mauritz Stiller; **Ph**: J. Julius; **Scr**: Ragnar Hyltén-Cavallius, Mauritz Stiller; **Cast**: Lars Hanson, Gerda Lundequist, Greta Garbo, Jenny Hasselqvist, Ellen Hortman-Cederström.

The Great Train Robbery
US, 1903 – 12 mins
Edwin S. Porter

It was the practice in the early days of cinema for one film-maker to copy the work of another, and it is essential that this be understood in the context of the times rather than being coloured by our current perceptions. Plagiarism belongs to the world of art or academic study and is frowned upon. But these short films were not great works of art or groundbreaking scientific discoveries; more akin to imitation in the fashion industry, any film that enjoyed commercial success was copied immediately. Direct copying, which is something you can do with film, *was* challenged and early producers peppered their prints with company brands to prevent unauthorised replication, just as we watermark our digital film files today, but the remake became common and acceptable. It is the film historian's fixation with 'firsts', and particularly the nationalist tendency in film history, that adds a pejorative tone to the copying of films at this time (are we somehow supposed to think better of ourselves because one of our countrymen apparently made some modest innovation in film-making technique?).

Perhaps it is time to think of early film-makers as developers and improvers rather than content thieves, and in this context Edwin S. Porter would reign supreme. His most popular film was *The Great Train Robbery* of 1903 – a work of original genius? No. It was based heavily on a British film released earlier that year called *Daring Daylight Burglary*, made in Sheffield by Frank Mottershaw, in which a small boy sees a burglar break into a house, alerts the police, who pursue the villain, one of whom is violently attacked and a dummy substituted as he is thrown from a high wall. Following a chase down a hill and across a stream, the burglar jumps onto a moving train, the policeman wires ahead and the villain is apprehended at the next station.

The film is shot in actual locations, which adds to the realist feel, and its similarities with *The Great Train Robbery* are immediately apparent.

The improvements that Porter made to this dramatic and very popular film (over a hundred prints were sent to America in early 1903) included changing the setting to the lawless West, building on the popularity of a play of 1896 and the publicity surrounding Butch Cassidy's notorious assault on the Union Pacific mail car in 1900. He spared no expense on the production, securing very fine shots of the train and inserting a fight scene as the bandits take over the engine (which is where the dummy shot occurs), while a matte shot of passing scenery through the window of the mail car greatly adds to the realism and judicious use of colour gives a three-dimensional feel. As an added attraction, the film concluded (or started) with an emblematic shot of the bandit leader shooting directly at the audience. What Porter does *not* do, however, contrary to much that you might read about this film, is to introduce cross-cutting. There are two sets of actions going on simultaneously – the rescue of a telegraph operator who has been forced by the bandits to send a false instruction to the train driver and then tied up, followed by his raising of the posse; and the train robbery itself. These scenes are told independently, with no intercutting of shots.

After the spectacular takings that Porter's film generated over Christmas 1903, it was copied in turn by Lubin, who added scenes of his own and undercut Edison's price. But if *The Great Train Robbery* is not quite the film-making milestone of dozens of dodgy internet entries, it certainly deserves a place in the canon for its sheer quality.

Dir: Edwin S. Porter; **Cast**: Georges Barnes, G. M. Anderson, Frank Hanaway, A. C. Abadie.

The Great White Silence
UK, 1924 – 106 mins
Herbert Ponting

The Great White Silence is one of many incarnations of the film shot by
Herbert Ponting in 1911 of Scott's *Terra Nova* expedition, demonstrating
the public's continuing interest in this tragic tale of adventure, bravery
and endurance. Antarctica was the last great continent left unexplored
by mankind. The early part of the twentieth century saw the 'heroic era'
of polar exploration, during which this incredibly hostile continent was
explored, measured and mapped, and the South Pole was finally
conquered. In 1910, the most famous polar expedition of them all set
out – the British Antarctic Expedition (1910–13), led by Captain Robert
Falcon Scott. With a complex (and completely genuine) scientific brief,
as well as an ambition to be the first to the Pole, the expedition also,
significantly, employed an official photographer and cinematographer,
Herbert Ponting, to document the journey. The conquest of the North
Pole had been disputed (and still is) due to the expedition's failure to
bring back any convincing proof. Amundsen, pipped to the post by Peary
for the North Pole, and hearing that Scott was about to set off for the
Antarctic, turned his ship around and headed south, not forgetting to
take a camera to ensure that the achievement was properly verifiable
and, of course, promotable. Media rights to memoirs, photographs and
footage had already begun to contribute very substantially to the funding
of an expedition.

   The films secured by Ponting in the first year of the expedition were
sold initially to Gaumont as reportage and then reissued in various forms.
When the disastrous news came through in 1913, Ponting edited his
footage together and went on a gruelling lecture tour to recoup money.
In 1924, after 2,000 appearances and encouraged perhaps by the
success of *Nanook of the North**, Ponting released *The Great White
Silence*, which, like his lecture, edited the material into a narrative of the
tragic events, introducing intertitles to explain the expedition footage,

as well as his own stills, maps, portraits and paintings. He even filmed
some novel sequences using elaborate models and stop-motion
photography to show the various journeys made by the polar teams.
The final film was tinted and toned to convey certain lighting effects.

The footage commences with the *Terra Nova*'s departure in 1910
from Lyttleton, on New Zealand's south island – a perilous journey during
which animals and stores were lost overboard in a gale and the ship had
to break through 400 miles of pack ice to reach the Great Ice Barrier.
Ponting took some of his most impressive footage, as he filmed the ship
breaking through the ice from a makeshift platform over the side.
Once they reached Ross Island, he filmed every aspect of the work of the
expedition, the scientific studies, life in camp and the local wildlife,
including killer whales, seals, Antarctic skuas and Adélie penguins.
The filming was in itself heroic. Ponting repeatedly risked frostbite in his
attempt to film and photograph in extremely cold temperatures.
Scott found Ponting's mastery of the art impressive and commented in
his diaries on his ability to endure the intense cold while standing still to
take photographs. Of course, the middle-aged Ponting would accompany
the expedition no further, but he did have the perspicacity to film Scott
and three others (interestingly, the same men who were to form the
polar team – Scott, Wilson, Evans and Bowers, though not Oates)
manhauling the sledge and cooking and sleeping in their tent, just as
they were to do on their way to the Pole. He could not have predicted
the tragic denouement – the polar team's crushing discovery that
Amundsen had beaten them to the Pole, and their terrible end in
unseasonably cold weather just 11 miles short of the depot of food
and fuel.

Dir/Ph: Herbert Ponting.

Greed
US, 1924 – 140 mins
Erich von Stroheim

In the ever-shifting negotiation between art and commerce in the rise of the Hollywood studios, there was one particularly unfortunate victim, Erich von Stroheim's *Greed*. It is particularly ironic that the theme of the film should be avarice, miserliness and murderous rage, as, on this occasion, money won. This adaptation of the great American novel *McTeague* by Frank Norris was to be von Stroheim's masterpiece, a work of naturalism and truth about human nature in the nation's burgeoning cities. The book is as crammed with detail as any Dickens novel and so compelling that it is easy to see why von Stroheim wanted passionately to do justice to it by giving it the appropriate scope. Although the characters are unlikeable, from the kindly but simple McTeague whose red-mist rages end in murder, to the spiteful Marcus and the miserly Trina, the realism is remarkable. I can't think of many films of the period, even in the truncated form in which *Greed* has survived, that gave me such a sense of what life was really like for the ordinary people of America. The realism has much to do with the authentic locations and incredible photography, but it is never short on drama either, with one of the best open endings in film history as McTeague and Marcus fight to the death in Death Valley.

The consensus of contemporary critical opinion was that von Stroheim's artistic hubris had finally run away with him and that he only had himself to blame if the studio butchered his film. Robert E. Sherwood, reviewing the 140-minute release version (which was all that was left of the original 10 hours) in *Life*, is cattily clear on this:

Ferocity, brutality, muscle, vulgarity, cruelty, naked realism and sheer genius are to be found – great hunks of them … It is a terribly powerful picture – and an important one. There are two defects in *Greed* – one of which is almost fatal. In the first place, von Stroheim has chosen to be symbolic at intervals, and has inserted some very bad handcoloring to emphasize the goldenness of gold. This detracts greatly from the realism of the picture. In the second place, von Stroheim has been, as usual, so extravagant with his footage that *Greed* in its final form is merely a series of remnants. It has been cut to pieces … This is von Stroheim's own fault … He is badly in need of a stopwatch.[12]

As most of the material that didn't make it into the badly abridged version has not survived, it is difficult to know how well this mammoth work would have played. A reconstruction using production stills and the original continuity script by Rick Schmidlin does fill in many of the gaps, but masterpiece or not, it can't have deserved this degree of cutting. There was no inherent reason why *Greed* could not have been released as a two-part film as they did in France (see *Monte Cristo**) except for the studio bosses' rigid mindset about exhibition practices. Marcus Loew always said, 'We sell tickets to theaters not movies', by which he meant that exhibitors essentially didn't care, as Richard Kozarski nicely puts it, 'about the part of the show that came in a can'.[13]

Dir: Erich von Stroheim; **Scr**: Erich von Stroheim, June Mathis; **Ph**: Ben F. Reynolds, William H. Daniels; **Sets**: Cedric Gibbons; **Cast**: Gibson Gowland, ZaSu Pitts, Jean Hersholt, Dale Fuller, Chester Conklin, Tempe Piggot, Sylvia Ashton.

The Heart of the World
Canada, 2000 – 6 mins
Guy Maddin

There is a new category of silent film, known in the film world as
'twenty-first-century silents'. They are films made not just in the style of
silent film but displaying some significant acquaintance with silent film
vernacular. Guy Maddin's *The Heart of the World* just squeaks in,
released in 2000 as part of a showcase of new Canadian film-making
talent at the Toronto Film Festival. What the festival programmers may
not have been expecting is this 6-minute love letter to silent cinema.

The film is a tour de force of silent technique principally referencing
Russian film of the 1920s, and tells the story of the beautiful Anna,
a 'state scientist' who has responsibility for the heart of the world.
From her mathematical calculations, 'triple checked', she infers that the
end is nigh – 'One', 'day', 'left' flashes up in titles as she warns the
world of its doom. She loves two brothers and cannot decide between
Nikolai, a youthful mortician, or Osip, an actor currently playing Christ in
the Passion. Her indecision begins to affect the health of the world's
heart and she succumbs to the seduction of a fat, leering industrialist
(the crucial moment represented by a phallic cannon spurting out gold
coins). The world is in cardiac arrest, and both brothers reel from some
kind of shock, buildings totter, crowds panic. Osip, in his role as Christ,
tries to calm the people; Nikolai's dead rise from their coffins.
Anna comes to her senses and decides to 'Save the World', and turns
on the industrialist. She strangles him before descending through the
Earth's arteries to its core and sacrificing herself to become the new
heart of the world. The crisis over, equilibrium returns. The spirit of
Anna, superimposed on the hearts of the people, heralds the dawn of
the 'Kino' world – screens, like banners, everywhere project images
of dancers, musicians and performers.

Not only does Maddin take as his subject silent cinema but
everything about the film-making, composition, design and editing

references it. The rapid editing – no shot lasts longer than a couple of seconds – recalls Vertov or Ruttmann, while the representation of the workings of Anna's mathematical brain by equations and diagrams resembles Abel Gance's *Napoleon**. The use of silhouettes to show sinister events is reminiscent of Segundo de Chomón's *Excursion incoherente* (1909) or DeMille's *The Cheat**. Maddin's employment of anamorphic lenses to distort scenery, the strong diagonals, the high and low angles, the use of representational types and symbolism, along with the solitary figure who addresses a crowd standing in for the whole world and the deployment of Anna as a kind of modernist earth goddess, all recall Eisenstein. Maddin's use of the intertitles – a few words writ large in the imperative – is pure Vertov, and, of course, the very concept of 'Kino' and the device of 'Kino Eye', with its circular iris, come directly from his films. The extra element of music that Maddin introduces would have been very much after Vertov's own heart: part of a piece composed back in the 1960s by Russian Georgi Sviridov, it integrates not only the impressionist sounds of the modernist machine age but also thematically links to the idea of progress – the title of the piece is *Time, Forward!* It is the use of the music, with its pile-driving rhythm, together with the rapid editing and indistinct monochrome photography, that opens this film up to a modern audience familiar with the 'industrial' aesthetic. The two works – film and music – operate perfectly on their own, but together they are dynamite. This is what prevents *The Heart of the World* from becoming merely pastiche or a *hommage*. As Maddin himself observed, 'Talkies weren't invented because there were no more silents to be made.'[14]

Dir/Scr/Ph: Guy Maddin; **Art Dir**: Olaf Dux; **Music**: Georgi Sviridov; **Cast**: Leslie Bais, Caelum Vatnsdal, Shaun Balbar, Greg Klymkiw.

Hell's Hinges
US, 1916 – 64 mins
Charles Swickard

Nearly everything in current cinema can be traced back to the silent era – including that most popular of genres we know as the Western. Its visual elements preceded the cinema in stage plays or the great touring extravaganzas like Buffalo Bill's Wild West Show, while the parameters of location, historical period and accoutrements were more or less set by the time film began to exploit its popularity. The history of the Western on film seems to have been a long trail towards authenticity. Considering that such a world barely existed in reality, the audience's desire for depictions of the Wild West is surprisingly tenacious. One of the key milestones along the way was the persona created by William S. Hart in a series of 'Westerns' made for Thomas Ince. Hart, in his late forties when he began to make films, had the weather-beaten looks appropriate for the Western hero and introduced a more naturalistic acting style which immediately made him stand out from the other actors, who were still employing a melodramatic approach. Fans of the classic and Clint Eastwood Western will recognise this type as the good bad man, a quiet loner with a past, no goody-goody certainly, but with a sound moral code and the ability to take command of a situation.

In *Hell's Hinges*, Hart's character, Blaze Tracy, is such a man. This is established as soon as the action reaches the eponymous town, 'a gun-fighting, man-killing, devil's den of iniquity that scorched even the sun-parched soil on which it stood'. A mob of unruly outlaws that congregate around 'Silk' Miller's saloon greet Blaze as their hero – a crack shot and a reckless rider, he can stop a crowd of drunken cowboys dead in their tracks by sheer force of character. But it is an alliance of convenience; he is not one of them. Ultimately, he turns away from the saloon towards the church, attracted by the virtuous and courageous young sister of the new pastor, as she tries to rally the small band of respectable citizens. In one of the best shots in the film, he reads the

Bible she has given him with apparent interest, fag in hand and whisky bottle at his elbow. The showdown comes when the bad guys, in a drunken spree, having ruined the easily tempted Reverend with whores and whisky, force him to set light to his own church. The flames of the burning church, tinted red in the film, are reflected on Blaze's face, evoking his fury when he finds the Reverend dead and his love distraught. His vengeance against the townspeople is as terrible as anything from the Old Testament. Having single-handedly razed the town to the ground, he stands impassively as the saloon burns around him, defying so much as a spark to drop on him.

It's the stuff of a thousand Westerns since, and although *Hell's Hinges* is still primarily a melodrama, it moves the genre along the road to greater realism. With its panoramic views of the deserts and canyons of the Western landscape, the film recreates not only the splendour but also the dust and sordidness of the old West, with its drunks, prostitutes and gunslingers.

Dir: Charles Swickard (William S. Hart, uncredited); **Scr**: C. Gardner Sullivan; **Ph**: Joseph August; **Cast**: William S. Hart, Clare Williams, Jack Standing, Louise Glaum, Alfred Hollingsworth.

Les Hôtes de l'air (*Glimpses of Bird Life*)

France, 1910 – 7 mins
Oliver Pike

Natural history films don't get a high profile in any but the most comprehensive film histories, but they should, for these are some of the most painstaking and rewarding of all film-making efforts. Sometimes taking years to make, these productions required more time and money than other films. It took a well-ordered and well-financed film company to undertake this kind of investment but the rewards could be great, as the films had a long shelf life. Big producers like Charles Urban in Britain and Pathé in France devoted considerable attention to wildlife films. Pathé headhunted British natural history pioneer Oliver Pike after he produced his own film *In Birdland* (1907), which played at the Palace Theatre in London for six weeks and sold 100 prints. Pathé contracted Pike to make several films with considerable investment, including beautifully subtle stencil colouring, for distribution all over the world. In his book *Nature and My Cine Camera* (Focal Press, 1946), Pike recalls a visit to the Pathé factory in Paris to see the elaborate stencilling process carried out by hundreds of skilled women workers, noting the accuracy of the colouring of the birds' plumage. In Pathé catalogues of the time, Pike is one of a very few featured directors, along with world-class names such as Albert Capellani and Segundo de Chomón.

Hôtes de l'air is a particularly good example of Pike's films for Pathé, as it captures birds in their natural habitat, his speciality. It includes a variety of seabirds and natives of the Farne Islands and of the Orkney and Shetland Islands. We see colonies of cliff-dwelling guillemots, gulls, puffins, gannets and land-dwelling sparrowhawks, baby buzzards, reed warblers, turtle doves and a cuckoo, as well as the hooded raven and the rare Richardson's Skua. The film still has the power to surprise the viewer with its beauty and groundbreaking techniques. In one sequence, we see a host of seagulls in mid-air, in itself an unusual shot in 1910, but Pike's positioning of the camera (on a corner of cliff where the birds had to fly into the wind) and adjusted focal plane make it feel years ahead of its time.

The English, it seems, had a natural propensity for the natural history film, producing several of the great pioneers in the field, Percy Smith, the Kearton brothers and Oliver Pike being the most notable. They seem to share several traits – a 'boy's own' passion for wildlife from an early age, technical inventiveness and competence, as well as physical stamina and courage. Underlying this was an absolute conviction that the public would want to see the resulting images as they were, without resort to anthropomorphism or overlying narrative. They were not wrong.

Nature films were very popular. Pathé knew what they were doing when they employed him, for Oliver Pike was no child prodigy. He had been pioneering natural history photography and cinematography from the late 1890s, having developed his own stills camera, the 'Birdland', cleverly baffled so as not to scare away the wildlife with the clunk of its shutter. The device was so good that it was bought by a London manufacturer, and Pike later adapted his cine cameras in the same way for wildlife cine-photography. But his significance lies not only in the groundbreaking techniques he developed to capture wildlife in its natural habitat but in the fact that he explained his techniques and methods in books and lectures for the next generation. His profound knowledge of photographic technique is evidenced by his handbooks on photography and cinematography, as well as his extant films.

This fostering of continual progress in technique and the pursuit of ever more daring exploits to capture images of the world's rarest wildlife has led directly to the pinnacles of achievement of later film-makers such as David Attenborough.

Dir/Ph: Oliver Pike; **Prod Co**: Pathé Frères.

How a Mosquito Operates
US, 1912 – 6 mins
Winsor McCay

Animation preceded 'real life' moving pictures by many years.
Drawings had been animated for optical toys for many decades before
film came on the scene, and conceptually, of course, strip cartoons are so
akin to film that it is surprising that cartoon artists were not making films
sooner. The reasons were primarily economic. Animating for film is
laborious and expensive, requiring not only a particular individualistic
vision and talent but also the patience of a saint. These are not virtues
that are commonly found together, so these pioneering animators were
rare and special people, and despite a number of early attempts – films
of lightning sketch artists, stop-motion and model animations, and the
drawn animations of Emile Cohl – it was not until around 1912 that
Ladislas Starewicz in Russia and Winsor McCay in the US, pursuing very
separate styles, brought together the narrative and characterisation that
would begin to demonstrate the real creative potential of animation.

McCay's *How a Mosquito Operates* is a quantum leap in animation
terms. It consists of a staggering 6,000 drawings, only occasionally
reusing looped sets of images for repeated actions. The story is very
simple: a man comes home and is pursued by an oversized top-hatted
mosquito clutching a valise. To the man, of course, the insect is tiny, as in
real life, and he bats it away as he turns over and over trying to get to
sleep. To us, with our privileged view, it is huge and we see in close-up
how it plunges its newly sharpened proboscis into the man's neck and
draws up blood. To add insult to injury, the mosquito is enjoying itself
(something we've always suspected), and as it begins to get bloated with
blood, it performs balancing tricks, consciously making eye contact (as it
were) with the audience – us – demanding applause. But as it indulges in
one more drink, it swells and swells, finally exploding with a bang,
blacking out the entire frame. It's funny, grotesque and brilliantly drawn
with astonishingly realistic movement.

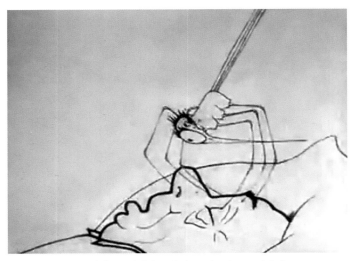

Man and mosquito eyeball to eyeball through the genius of cartoonist/animator
Winsor McCay

Winsor McCay was a great artist whose few films are just a minor
part of his extraordinary legacy. Early training had taught him not only
how to draw perspective accurately but also to scrutinise perspective.
In his strip cartoons, such as *Little Nemo in Slumberland* and *Dream of a
Rarebit Fiend*, he drew from every angle and point of view playing with
scale, speed and flights of fancy that would leave Lewis Carroll and
L. Frank Baum standing. He was a big influence on film before he ever
made one – compare his *Little Sammy Sneeze* strip with Hepworth's *That
Fatal Sneeze* (1907), and, of course, there was Edwin Porter's direct steal,
Dreams of a Rarebit Fiend (1906). McCay was also a performer, touring
with a live act as a lightning sketch artist, who used his films interactively
and could be said to have invented film perfomance art. His most famous
film, *Gertie the Dinosaur* (1914), was part of a live act in which McCay
would converse with the animated dinosaur from the stage and she

would respond. For the grand finale, he would appear on screen with her. *How a Mosquito Operates* was also used in the live act and, like McCay's first film, *Little Nemo* (1911), would have had a live-action prologue for theatrical release, which unfortunately seems to be lost. For those who think the cinematic graphic novel began with Allan Moore's *Watchmen*, they should look at McCay's work eighty years previously.

Dir/Anim: Winsor McCay.

I Was Born, But … (Otona no miru ehon – umarete wa mita keredo)
Japan, 1932 – 100 mins
Yasujiro Ozu

I have never heard of anyone who has seen this film who didn't love it. It is *very* funny without being a comedy and has that indefinable verisimilitude that characterises the best writers and directors. It is also acutely observed, perfectly paced and packs a punch. The lightness of touch in the earlier scenes contrasts sharply with the climax, so that by the end you feel you have weathered an emotional storm. Subtitled 'A picture-book for grown-ups', the film's themes are generational conflict told from the child's point of view and 'face' – i.e. who stands up to who, and wins.

The story revolves principally around two young boys, ten and eight years old, who, being new in the neighbourhood, have to square up to the local gang headed by a large bully and the son of their father's boss. Bizarre rituals define the status of a particular gang member, where the stronger boy is allotted the power to immobilise the weaker ones with a gesture of the hand, leaving them lying flat on the ground till released. This is reflected in their father's office workplace, where status is exhibited in much the same manner, with the father kowtowing to his boss in order to 'get on'. The elder boy, like a little Napoleon, having conquered the playground and established himself as top dog, is mortified when, at a screening of the boss's home movies, he and his brother see their father clowning for his rich employer's amusement. This loss of face is unbearable and leads to a full-on tantrum in which he calls his father a weakling. The little one mirrors everything that his brother does, and in another face-off between the boys and their parents, they refuse to eat until, of course, hunger gets the better of them and reason can be re-established. The father wisely elects not to explain to them that he does what he does to provide them with the benefits of a nice neighbourhood and education that his generation never had but instead asks the younger boy what he wants to be when he grows up – a lieutenant general, he says. 'Why not a full general?' his father asks, but the answer is obvious – naturally, the elder brother will take this rank, and so the natural pecking order reasserts itself. As father and sons walk – they to school and he to the office – they encounter the boss in his car. To show his sons that he doesn't need to kowtow, the father casually ignores the boss. But the boys become increasingly embarrassed by his refusal to acknowledge his superior, and eventually the eldest caves in. 'You'd better go and say hello to him Dad.' The little smile his father gives him indicates that he has been forgiven, peace reigns and everyone goes off to start the new day.

As with all Ozu films, the microcosm of the family drama contains within it profound truths about human behaviour. Everything about the film-making process underpins the development of the story. First, there is the structure, with its repeated set-ups (such as the morning journey to

After the storm … father and two sons are reconciled with rice balls

school), similar but different each time as the tension builds; then there is the acting, which is phenomenal, particularly from the two boys (Tomio Aoki, the younger, 'funny looking kid', was still acting on screen in 2004); while most interesting perhaps for those unfamiliar with Japanese cinema is the low-level camerawork reinforcing the child's perspective. As a late silent film, it is a masterwork, although you can feel that the director desperately wants to include dialogue (there is a significant build-up of intertitles during the climactic scene), which leads me to conclude that the high level of sophistication in Japanese film-making was well established surprisingly early on.

Dir: Yasujiro Ozu; **Scr**: Akira Fushimi; **Ph**: Hideo Mohara; **Cast**: Tatsuo Saito, Hideo Sugawara, Tokkan Kozou (Tomio Aoki), Mitsuko Yoshikawa.

L'Inferno
Italy, 1911 – 14 mins (of 21)
Giuseppe Beradi, Arturo Busnego

Almost all of the elements of early film exhibition, and the direction cinema would take next, could be hung off this one film. A pirate version, made by the Helios company just outside Rome, of Dante's *L'Inferno*, and one of the earliest 'feature' films, exclusive or super-productions, as they were variously known, it heralded in a new era of film exhibition and competition recognisable in the cinema of today. The year 1911 was an interesting one for the consolidation of the cinema as a serious business: regular newsreels were launched and huge amounts were invested in super-productions that could be released exclusively to exhibitors at premium prices. Several versions of almost identical productions were produced in this year. Marketing became cut-throat. In this press notice, we can see how the distributor is pushing the Milano version of the 'Inferno' above its rivals:

> This masterpiece is 5,000ft long … a treasure for six hundred years, known to but a few scholars, now placed in unsurpassable beauty before all mankind; presented by the film-makers just as conceived by the immortal Poet, occupying about two hours, telling in the most artistic and realistic manner the great story of DANTE like animated paintings of living statuary. The pictures give you in a few hours all the pleasure and knowledge it takes months to acquire through books, consequently the chance of a lifetime … Beware of imitations.'[15]

This piece of marketing puff illustrates many features of early cinema, including the fairground showmanship, the cinema of spectacle and the appropriation of artworks – Dante's famous fourteenth-century narrative poem and Gustave Doré's illustrations for Dante's *Divine Comedy* of 1861. It references antiquity, statuary and painting – kitemarks of quality – while at the same time advertising it as an innovation, and

suggesting the aspirational and elevating educational benefits.
The implication is that you would be able to 'bluff-your-way in Dante's
Inferno' after watching this film, and, with infernal cheek, suggests that
Dante himself would have approved. It is ironic, then, that this innovatory
film should now be, like the classical statuary that informs the design,
a fragmentary relic itself, battered and incomplete.

The Milano version mentioned in the notice above eventually
prevailed over the Helios version – it was longer, which helped, and
contained more nudity. But the shorter Helios version has an energy
about it which in some ways makes it more watchable and, despite
being regarded as the pirated film, it was actually released first.
Both versions are very faithful renditions of the text, starting with Dante's
meeting with Virgil and their descent into hell. Here the film follows the
cantos, detailing the various torments devised for particular categories of
sinner and exploiting the opportunity to show off some great special
effects: a wonderful matte shot for the infernal hurricane of lustful souls,
a clever effect made by scratching the emulsion from the film to
represent the molten rock that rains down on the blasphemers and novel
use of sets showing the Simonists buried head down in fiery pits with
only their writhing feet exposed. The film is beautifully tinted, making full
use of blazing red to convey the heat of the inferno and of blue-green to
convey the cold of the frozen core of hell where Lucifer sits munching on
the live bodies of traitors. No one ever lost money with tales of the Devil.

Dir: Giuseppe Beradi, Arturo Busnego; **Cast**: Giuseppe Beradi, Armando Novi.

The Informer
UK, 1929 – 83 mins
Arthur Robison

Liam O'Flaherty's 1925 novel of the same name was adapted twice for the screen, famously in 1935 by John Ford. This earlier version produced in sound and silent versions is arguably better. One of the finest films produced in a British studio in the 1920s, it can scarcely claim to be British at all. With a German director and cinematographer, a Hungarian leading lady and Swedish leading man, this is a truly European effort. But, in fact, this level of international collaboration was typical of the late silent period, particularly in Europe. Films from these years, now known as 'international' films by film historians, were made specifically to appeal to multiple markets in different languages and drew on talent from all over the world.

British International Pictures, one of the largest studios in England, brought over Arthur Robison from Germany where he had famously directed *Schatten* (1923), now considered a classic of German Expressionism. With him came German cinematographer Werner Brandes, who had worked with Fritz Lang and who was responsible for giving *The Informer* its distinctively dark and claustrophobic look. A good-looking and talented cast led by Lars Hanson combined to lend intensity to this tale of personal betrayal during the aftermath of the Irish rebellion of 1916.

Filmed nearly all in mid-shot and close-up to give it a cramped feel, *The Informer* was entirely photographed in the studio, although the design is so good that you might almost believe you were in Dublin. It is not without movement – a particularly fine tracking shot takes you from a rooftop down through the bustling street, past a cinema to ground level and follows the central character, Gypo (Hanson), as he elbows his way through the crowd in a jealous rage on his way to inform on his friend and co-revolutionary. The cinematography perfectly serves the theme of the narrative, which

WARDOUR *presents*
LARS HANSEN & LYA DE PUTTI *in* "THE INFORMER" A BRITISH INTERNATIONAL PICTURE.
directed by **DR. A. ROBISON**

The shadow of the Law falls on Carl Harbord's Irish fugitive

pivots on the question of personal redemption in a world without possible escape. What gives the film its tension is the fact that it is set in almost real time. With the exception of the opening scenes, the action takes place in a day and a night. This temporal device engages the viewer's attention closely as the events of the story unfold, and it enables the central actors to portray the reactions of the characters with a degree of naturalism that they appear to experience simultaneously with the audience.

All three lead characters deliver beautifully restrained performances. It is a testament to the acting skill of Hanson that he can convey a series of complex emotions in a situation that would make a villain of a lesser character. This is borne out by the judgment of his girlfriend in the story, Kate, played by Lya de Putti, who can forgive Gypo the considerable sin of informing on a comrade, even for the ignoble reason that he was jealous of her supposed feelings for this comrade. It is not the damnation of his actions by his peers that destroys him in the end but his condemnation of himself.

Dir: Arthur Robison; **Ph**: Werner Brandes, T. Sparkuhl; **Cast**: Lya de Putti, Lars Hanson, Warwick Ward, Carl Harbord.

It
US, 1927 – 72 mins
Clarence Badger

'It', 'it' or 'IT', as you will find it variously listed, is as quintessentially 1920s as *The Great Gatsby* if only a few notches further down the social scale. Without Clara Bow, it would be a pleasant if somewhat thinly plotted romantic comedy, but *with* her, it becomes a film you can hang a decade on. The bobbed hairstyle, the cloche hats, cupid's bow lips, the fast cars, yachts and Coney Island funfairs were the outer trappings, but there was an indefinable mood about the 1920s which all had to do with the city, breaking away from the previous generation, freedom, youth, success, mobility and materialism. Central to one's success in the 1920s was 'It'. Elinor Glyn, author of the original story, defined 'It' as 'that quality possessed by some which draws all others with its magnetic force. With IT you win all men if you are a woman – all women if you are a man.' The expression has been common currency ever since, as far as it applies to women.

Clara Bow, who plays Betty Lou, a department-store shop girl who has sworn to marry the boss, clearly has 'It'. We know this because the silly-ass friend Monty (William Austin) carries a copy of Glyn's story in an issue of *Cosmopolitan* round the store eyeing up the girls for signs of the magical quality. When he spots Betty Lou, he recognises it straightaway, and when Betty Lou sees the boss, Cyrus Waltham (Antonio Moreno), she detects something in him too. She positively purrs 'Sweet Santa Claus, give me him!' Whereas we are in no doubt whatsoever that Clara Bow has 'It' in spades, it is never made explicit whether Waltham does, which is just as well, because Moreno seems rather to have that quality possessed by some which draws a total blank. There is a good deal of comedy in the fact that initially he doesn't see her at all. But none of this matters, because when Clara Bow is on the screen, you can't look at anything else. She is mesmerising, vivacious, flirty without being worryingly sexy, kittenish and adorable.

Flapper extraordinaire, the adorable Clara Bow defines 'It'

The sequence where she takes Waltham to taste the proletarian pleasures of Coney Island seems entirely designed to reveal more of her than would normally be on show. That glimpse of stocking tops and satin knickers may have been more shocking in 1927 but I suspect not, and neither is very much else in the film. Betty Lou is refreshingly feisty on behalf of a downtrodden friend who is being harassed by do-gooders trying to deprive her of her baby. Betty claims the baby is her own, which is the root of the misunderstanding that leads to Waltham offering her

protection short of marriage. She is rightly outraged, for like Millie in
Thoroughly Modern Millie (1967), a pastiche of the Roaring Twenties
partly based on 'It', Betty Lou is really a nice old-fashioned girl. It is left to
the silly-ass friend to put things straight, but not before she has had a
chance to deliver a spirited left hook to Waltham's ladylike fiancée –
described as 'one of' eighteen million blondes. The blonde is left with
'It'-less Monty and the 'It' girl gets her man.

Dir: Clarence Badger; **Scr**: Hope Loring, Louis D. Lighton; **Ph**: H. Kinley Martin; **Cast**: Clara
Bow, Antonio Moreno, William Austin, Jacqueline Gadsden.

Japonaiseries
France, 1904 – 4 mins
Gaston Velle

The thriving entertainment industry of the *belle époque* was a great maelstrom of attractions, spectacles and diversions delivered through the fairgrounds or the great music halls and theatres of the city. Accompanying these shows was a cacophony of advertising, images and words in a kind of print version of the fairground barker, all designed to entice you in. No wonder then that when film arrived as the latest novelty – one 'act' among so many – it should fit itself into the existing exhibition structure and co-opt its most popular commodities. Of these, the most sensational was magic. Magic shows were hugely popular and had migrated from the touring fairs to specialised theatres in the great cities of Europe. Film was at first seen by some professional magicians as a bit of magic paraphernalia used to enhance their stage tricks, but soon film-makers were incorporating magic within the film itself. Inspired by films of celebrated magicians like Maskelyne and Davenant in London, Georges Méliès began to include his own magic shows in his films, spawning a whole genre of film that would prove successful for a decade. It was he, primarily, who combined stage and photographic trickery, retaining the persona and performance style of the magician but using the camera to effect tricks that would be impossible to achieve on the stage.

From the late 1890s, these films were made in profusion by many of the film companies but the Paris producers dominated. When the Pathé company began to expand their film business, they naturally looked for ways to compete with Méliès, and hired professionals such as Gaston Velle to make *scènes a trucs*. Velle was an illusionist and son of an illusionist who had an act in Italy and Paris, so hiring him away from his regular act had the additional benefit to the company of reducing the competition.

Japonaiseries is a simple trick film that incorporates a Japanese setting, with elaborate painted backdrops in the oriental style (enhanced by the beautiful stencil colouring which Pathé specialised in). On a stage set up within a proscenium, the magician performs a series of tricks with the aid of a magic box. What is interesting, and only really observable if you can stop and advance the film a frame at a time, is that he uses, almost unnecessarily, some stage machinery as well as the photographic techniques. When the magician appears out of his magic box, it is through a 'star trap' in the stage floor – a type of trapdoor system which propels the actor at some velocity upwards through a door made up of hinged flaps (in a star shape), which then fall back into place as the actor lands on the stage. The next trick, in which the magician makes a lovely young 'Japanese' girl appear, is achieved by a straightforward cut, stopping the camera and introducing the girl. By 1904, this would have been completely apparent to the audience used to seeing films, but everything moves along at a smart pace, as a good magic act should. The final trick (in the somewhat truncated print) is trick cinema at its best. The magician pulls a number of little cubes out of his magic box and constructs a wall, which he knocks down and then reassembles magically by waving his magic fan (shot in reverse). As the wall reassembles, it forms a picture of a living child, who throws kisses to the audience; the procedure is repeated but this time with an image of the Pathé cockerel, serving as a useful copyright brand. It is beautifully done and works even with modern audiences, for whom it has the added novelty of age.

Dir: Gaston Velle; **Prod Co**: Pathé Frères.

The Kid
US, 1921 – 68 mins
Charles Chaplin

There are some directors for whom it has been especially difficult to
choose only one or two examples of their work. Chaplin is one.
So, disregarding favourites or classics, I've gone for *The Kid*, because it is
a pivotal film in his career marking the end of one set of films and the
beginning of another. It also tells you a lot about Chaplin, his
background, his philosophy of life and relationships with others. *The Kid*
is atypical of Chaplin films for a number of reasons: it was his first
feature, and after completing three more shorts for his First National
contract, he would make only feature-length films; he also would part
company with his leading lady of seven years, Edna Purviance; and it was
the only time he shared the billing with another performer, the child
actor Jackie Coogan. In other ways, *The Kid* is Chaplin's most personal
film and perhaps he made it to lay some old ghosts about his
upbringing, which like the kid's and little tramp's was full of poverty and
uncertainty. Although in an American setting, it closely resembles the
London of Chaplin's youth, an environment peopled with criminal gangs
and unsympathetic authority where abandoned children were left to
subsist by petty thievery and home was a shabby garret.

In the film, Chaplin 'adopts' the abandoned baby of the title, and a
good deal of the comedy arises from his improvised and ingenious
methods of looking after the infant with the meagre resources to hand
(a coffee pot suspended from the ceiling does duty as a feeding bottle).
And when the kid has grown a little, their quite sophisticated domestic
arrangements (the kid expertly cooking Sunday morning pancakes and
nagging at Charlie to get up and eat his breakfast like any housewife)
show the proper respect for more bourgeois values of table manners and
cleanliness, however poor they may be. The child, however, is also
suitably streetwise, brandishing a quarter for the meter on a string, and
has a good aim with a half-brick. In a scheme to make ends meet, the

kid breaks windows, while Charlie, the peripatetic glazier, is conveniently at hand to repair them. When the two are separated by the authorities, it is genuinely harrowing. Again, this may reflect Chaplin's personal memories of being dragged forcibly away from his mother and half-brother at a young age, but he had also lost a child just before making the film and the desperation is palpable.

There is one scene – a dream sequence – that is sometimes ambiguous for the modern audience. In fact, it is a throwback to the pantomime harlequinade of Chaplin's childhood, in which a transformation takes place: in this case, the tramp, falling asleep, dreams that the horrible slum becomes a paradise with enough to eat for all, where the bullies and even the dog transfigure into white-robed, winged angels and the streets are festooned with flowers. So here again, Chaplin seems to be reliving his past. It was shortly after completion of the film that an exhausted and homesick Chaplin went back to London for the first time in nine years.

Dir/Scr/Prod: Charles Chaplin; **Ph**: Roland Totheroh; **Cast**: Charles Chaplin, Jackie Coogan, Edna Purviance, Charles Reisner, Jackie Coogan Sr.

(*Opposite page*) 'He's behind you!': British pantomime traditions are subtly transposed to the screen through the art of Charlie Chaplin

Lenin Kino-Pravda No. 21 (Leninskaia Kino-Pravda)
USSR, 1925 – 30 mins
Dziga Vertov

In the opening titles of *Man with a Movie Camera**, Vertov states his
intention to create a truly international language of cinema, separate
from the language of theatre or literature – an experiment without the
aid of story or intertitles. His earlier work on the newsreel series
'Kino-Pravda' ('cinema truth') was, by contrast, crammed with intertitles.
These were not the simple explanatory titles of regular western newsreels
but were conceived and used creatively in the cause of Vertov's own
brand of Soviet propaganda. They were based on collaborations with
Alexei Gan and Aleksander Rodchenko, both of whom were committed
Constructivists who shunned 'art for art's sake' in favour of art in the
service of progress and the Revolution, much of which centred on
graphic design. The words themselves were written by Vertov in both a
declamatory and oratorical style based on a passion for poetry. In fact,
Vertov was a kind of artistic synaesthete, passionately interested in all
kinds of interactions – poetry and graphics, sound and music, and the
moving image – while at the same time rejecting others, such as fine art
and fiction, in pursuit of truth. He argued with the critics after *Battleship
Potemkin** had been hailed as a 'rejuvenated art drama', fighting for his
newsreel as the real representative of Lenin's legacy:

> Therefore direct your rapture to the correct address. This address is
> 24 Tverskaia Street Moscow, a basement half flooded with water where
> we *Kinocs* work … don't look at the flowers comrades, look at the root
> … here comrades new forms of film production are being constructed,
> here every step is an invention, every metre shot is a search, every
> edited piece an experiment, every film-thing is an arduous struggle and
> a victory.[16]

Lenin Kino-Pravda No. 21 was made towards the end of this newsreel project to celebrate the first anniversary of the death of Lenin in January 1924. Composed of actuality newsreel re-edited with the aid of titles and graphics, it follows the three-part Marxist paradigm of thesis, antithesis and synthesis, starting with the assassination attempt on Lenin by Fanny Kaplan in 1918 which weakened his health, moving on to his illness and death, and ending with the legacy of Leninism. The key scene at Lenin's lying-in-state, even though it is made up of reused footage, is very powerful. The mourners include the members of the Central Committee, Lenin's wife and sister, representatives of all the soviets, and, of course, the masses. It is here that Vertov uses the gloriously blocky fonts in different sizes to emphasise importance: the word 'Lenin' fills the frame as, later, does the word 'Masses'. Of the other attendees, only Stalin's name is the same size. That poetic tendency is also revealed here in the titles 'Lenin … but he is motionless'/'Lenin … but he is silent', contrasting markedly with the initial section of the film, in which he is seen constantly speaking, energetically exhorting the masses to carry on the work of the Revolution. As the mourners file past his embalmed body, the titles grow in size: '200,000, 400,000, 700,000'. The refrain is repeated: 'The masses are moving'/'The masses are silent'.

The relationship between the masses and the leader is the essential one – 'Lenin is dead but his strength is with us' it says, as we watch the work of Leninism going on in the factories and fields, and in the education, machine building and electrification projects. The final shot is of a train rushing forward 'on the road of Leninism – full speed ahead'.

Dir: Dziga Vertov.

Liberty
US, 1929 – 20 mins
Leo McCarey

There is a scene in Peter Bogdanovich's 1976 film *Nickelodeon* (which anyone interested in silent film should watch, if only to have fun spotting all the references) in which ex-lawyer Leo Harrigan is caught up with a bunch of movie people in 1910s New York – the studio boss is brainstorming ideas for their next picture and Harrigan is desperately trying to pass himself off as a scriptwriter while the cast and crew chip in. They have just come up with a plot of sorts when one of the actors adds 'and he has a crab in his pants!' I remember wondering about that little detail, but it was not till years later that I saw the film it came from – a Laurel and Hardy silent called *Liberty* and one of their best.

Stan and Ollie play escaped convicts who have changed into civvies at haste, only to realise that they have each other's pants on – they try unsuccessfully to swap trousers in various locations while evading the police. It is during their last attempt, round the back of a fish shop, that the crab gets into Ollie's trousers. In the next scene, they arrive at a building site and step backwards into the site elevator that takes them to the top of a skyscraper under construction – the lift descends and the boys are left clinging desperately to the girders. As they inch their way precariously towards a ladder, with Stan a gibbering wreck, the crab (of course) comes into play. Everything that should be safe and solid – a rope, a ladder and even the steel girders themselves – proves to be completely unreliable. It's a dazzling tour de force of the gag-writer's art.

Thirty-three of Laurel and Hardy's hundred or so films together were silent and, as they are made more available, are becoming appreciated for the classics they are. *Liberty* is one of a large number of short comedies produced in the later silent era; known as two-reelers, they run at about 20 minutes or so (typically, a reel of 35mm film is 1,000ft long and lasts about 10 minutes). The two-reeler is still very much with us but not in the cinema – 20–30 minutes is still the optimum running time for television comedy. In fact, this comedy format jumped from cinema to radio and thence to TV. One of the greatest creators of the two-reeler was writer/director Leo McCarey, who has been rehabilitated as an auteur in recent years, and worked for many years at the Hal Roach Studios under ideal conditions with a good deal of creative freedom. A natural delegator, McCarey allowed talent to thrive. No mean talent himself, he would play piano to the cast and crew while they improvised gags. Charley Chase, Max Davidson and Stan Laurel were all given their head by McCarey to make some of the funniest comedies ever made, including *Mighty Like a Moose* (1926), *Pass the Gravy* (1928) and *Should Married Men Go Home?* (1928), to name a few. This early training led McCarey to pursue a spectacular feature-film career that included some of Hollywood's best-loved films (*The Awful Truth* [1937], *An Affair to Remember* [1957]).

Roy Seawright, an effects technician at the Hal Roach Studios, remembered:

> I always look back to the days when things were kind of quiet, when they'd roll a piano over to Stage One, and Leo McCarey would start playing … And just like that, Charley Chase, Babe Hardy, Stan Laurel and Leo would start a quartet … You'd walk in and listen to them, and you'd be entranced … People would just flock around that stage. … They were completely free to express themselves. And that expression – that freedom – was manifested in their pictures.[17]

Dir/Scr: Leo McCarey; **Ph**: George Stevens; **Cast**: Stan Laurel, Oliver Hardy, James Finlayson.

The Lodger: A Story of the London Fog
UK, 1926 – 96 mins
Alfred Hitchcock

'It is possible that this film is the finest British production ever made,' said *The Bioscope* of 16 September 1926. After a bit of script doctoring, this was the verdict on *The Lodger: A Story of the London Fog*, Hitchcock's first suspense film and his first critical success. A couple of month's earlier, C. M. Woolf, the man in charge of distribution for Gainsborough, apparently had a contrary view: 'Your picture is so dreadful, that we're just going to put it on the shelf and forget about it,' he said, although it seems probable that he had been swayed by the jealous persuasions of Graham Cutts, who had till that time been the studio's top director. The picture was 'fixed' at the request of Michael Balcon by Ivor Montagu, who tightened up the intertitles and employed Britain's best graphic designer, E. McKnight Kauffer (significantly, like Montagu, a founder member of the Film Society), to give the film a modernist look. His triangular deco design, intended to invoke the love triangle of the main characters, was fully incorporated from the opening animated title and also featured in the calling card left by the 'Avenger' and the map of London on which the police are delineating their search area.

No doubt this artistic flourish enhances the film's modern look and was in keeping with the German films that Hitchcock had come to admire on his recent visit to Gainsborough's German partner, Ufa. In fact, it was entirely in keeping with the look that the director had already created, despite the Victorian setting of the source novel by Marie Belloc Lowndes. Hitchcock, or more likely Eliot Stannard, who adapted it, updated the story while retaining the fog. Ivor Novello, the quintessentially 1920s man, starred as the mysterious lodger who is suspected of being the Avenger, a serial killer of blonde girls. He falls for the landlady's daughter, Daisy (blonde, of course), but despite his gentlemanly manners, her mother becomes increasingly troubled by his strange behaviour, his violent reaction to the pictures of blonde women in his room, the midnight walks – in a wonderfully suspenseful visualisation of sound, she sees the lodger's feet superimposed on the ceiling pacing up and down, up and down. The book's original ending had to be altered, as a star like Novello couldn't be allowed to die. So, a dramatic pursuit by a mob bent on revenge supplies the climax, with the innocent hero hung Christ-like from some iron railings.

There are many features of *The Lodger* that became characteristic of Hitchcock's later films: the building of suspense, the stylistic use of montage shots and unusual camera angles, the use of sound (visualised in his silent films, made brilliantly actual in his sound films), the incorporation of words as pictures, handcuffs, mistaken identity, the chase and, of course, the cameo appearance. Every detail is planned and deliberate, the product of a master film-maker in waiting.

Dir: Alfred Hitchcock; **Scr**: Eliot Stannard; **Ph**: Baron Ventimiglia; **Cast**: Ivor Novello, June, Marie Ault, Arthur Chesney, Malcolm Keen.

The Lure of Crooning Water
UK, 1920 – 84 mins
A. H. Rooke

The films of Guy Newall and Ivy Duke, made in the very early 1920s,
seem to be an anomaly in British film history. These simple character-
driven dramas, primarily shot on location in rural settings, are beautifully
photographed and characterised by the naturalistic acting that owed a
debt to Ibsen and Strindberg, and to André Antoine, the influential
French theatre producer turned film director. Newall, particularly, was
celebrated for his minimalist acting style and was often referred to as
'Britain's best actor'. He had been on the stage since a youth and could
turn his hand to broad comedy or the more melancholic loner type that
featured in the series of films he made with producer George Clark at
the cramped Ebury Street studios in London. *Fox Farm* (1922) *Testimony*
(1920), *The Garden of Resurrection* (1919) and, most poignantly, *The
Lure of Crooning Water* could be seen as a development of Antoine's
French pastoral films. The acting style that Antoine aspired to was
achieved in the more intimate setting of the English countryside, while
the smaller storylines and closer camerawork allowed it to mature. At the
end of the 1920s, French directors such as Jean Epstein and Grémillon
would meld this naturalism with their own toned-down Impressionist
techniques to produce some very fine films, such as *Maldone* (1928)
(Newall is reminiscent of lead actor Charles Dullin) or the Breton series.
Poor Guy Newall could never have hoped to reach these heights on his
tiny budgets but the promise was there. Rachael Low, hardly one to go
mushy over a British talent, expresses real regret that Newall couldn't
take his directorial career further. His company was a victim of the
mid-1920s crisis in the British film industry.

The story is a little like *Sunrise**. Ivy Duke plays Georgette, a
glamorous but jaded city actress who is sent to the country by her
doctor/friend for a rest cure, where she causes married farmer Horace
(Guy Newall) to fall in love with her – because she can. The tensions

STOLL FILM C° L^TD   THE LURE OF CROONING WATER

Passions are unleashed as city sophisticate Ivy Duke cracks married farmer Guy
Newall's resolve

between the hard work and simple morals of the rural environment and
the excesses of the metropolis are thrown into sharp relief when he later
follows her to the city (of course, this being England, he makes no
attempt, as in *Sunrise*, to drown his wife in a lake). Restraint is the
watchword here. *The Bioscope* reviewer said that Ivy Duke's charms held
'just that touch of refinement and distinction that might cause
resentment in a village', and she does indeed play the part with great
subtlety, balancing her reckless flirting with the melancholy of a woman
profoundly weary of being used by men.

The setting up of the romance starts lightly – they hate each other
on sight. She sneers at his coarseness and he shows his disapproval of
her frivolity as she lounges about in a hammock teaching the baby to
smoke. This is juxtaposed with the homeliness and drudgery of Horace's

wife, Rachel (Mary Dibley), although husband and wife seem to have existed together happily enough till now. The pivotal scene takes place in a thunderstorm, prefigured metaphorically (or meteorologically) in an intertitle: 'Rachel didn't see the storm clouds gathering'. As Rachel comforts the children upstairs, Georgette opportunistically invades the farmer's private study. As the lightning flashes, he sarcastically asks if she is afraid. 'No,' she smoulders, 'I want someone to *revel* in it with me.' Bodies move closer, he follows her off screen and everything fades to black. That splendid electricity must have been real, as Duke and Newall married soon after.

Dir: A. H. Rooke; **Scr**: Guy Newall, from the novel by Marion Hill; **Ph**: C. J. Rosenthal; **Cast**: Ivy Duke, Guy Newall, Mary Dibley, Hugh C. Buckler.

Man with a Movie Camera (Chelovek s kinoapparatom)
USSR, 1929 – 68 mins
Dziga Vertov

Yuri Tsivian, in his brilliant DVD commentary on *Man with a Movie Camera* (which I cannot recommend highly enough – it could save you literally years of head-scratching), sums up by quoting critic Noël Burch's thoughts on the film:

> This film is not made to be viewed only once. It is impossible for anyone to assimilate its work in a single viewing ... it is resolutely reflexive – this film was the most radical gesture that the silent cinema had known ... there is not a single shot in the entire film that is not over-determined by whole sets of intertwined chains of signification.[18]

I wish someone had told me this before I saw it for the first time – I found it enjoyable enough to watch, like any of the city symphony films, with its dawn-to-dusk structure, its themes of work, lifecycle, leisure, transport and human/machine production. I understood some of the observations being drawn about life in these modern Russian cities (Moscow, Kiev, Yalta, Odessa), through clever juxtaposition, and was dazzled by the range of cinematic techniques on display and the fierce intelligence behind it. I had seen and admired the witty self-reflexive intrusions of the camera and the cameraman (played by Vertov's cinematographer brother Mikhail Kaufman) and the framing device of the movie show – but I didn't *really* get it. Fourth time round, I'm beginning to.

A first clue to unpacking *Man with a Movie Camera* occurs in the opening foreword to the film: 'this experimental work aims at creating a truly international absolute language of cinema based on its total separation from the language of theatre and literature'. This refers us to Vertov's manifesto contained within his 'Provisional Instructions to Kino-Eye Groups' of 1926, which was a blueprint for a very different kind of cinema and one that would not only create a visual Esperanto but would democratise film-making and lead to the essential recording of things that 'should not be forgotten' and 'what will have to be taken account of in the future'. Essentially, the instructions to the 'kinocs' suggest an equivalent of Baconian deductive reasoning – instead of working from a scenario, they would collect and collate film according to a theme and make their observations in the editing process. Vertov was concerned with the effect the camera had on the people he was filming and its corresponding effect on the 'truth' of the work. He devised several strategies for dealing with this, from simply accepting people's reactions (as Tsivian puts it, 'Life caught unawares'), to minimising people's awareness of the camera by hiding it – setting up decoy fake cameras or simply shooting from a distance with a telephoto lens ('Life as it is').

Underpinning this was an assumption that what you see with this 'kino eye' will impart some truth, but as Vertov notes, 'It is far from simple to show the truth, yet the truth is simple.' To draw out this truth, the process of editing and analysis must take place. In the film this is done by three figures: the invisible film-maker (Vertov himself), the cameraman (his brother, Mikhail) and the editor (Elizaveta Svilova, Vertov's wife). It is not only the cameraman who interacts with the film but also the editor, so that it is always both a film and its own 'making of'. Svilova is seen cutting the film, reordering shots that we then see on the screen, lining up the rolls thematically, followed by scenes of the cameraman shooting these very sequences. Her work is juxtaposed with images of women and machines, sewing, stitching and weaving, so that the film celebrates both the industry of the proletariat and the work of the film-maker in concert. Film-making becomes a task like any other piece of modern machine production, the duty of every citizen – creating a complex, useful and beautiful work. Coming right at the end of the silent era, *Man with a Movie Camera* shows us everything that film can do and everything that the cinema ought to become.

Dir: Dziga Vertov; **Ph**: Mikhail Kaufman; **Asst Ed**: Elizaveta Svilova.

Manhatta
US, 1921 – 7 mins
Charles Sheeler, Paul Strand

Photographers turned film-makers Charles Sheeler and Paul Strand
produced this short film of a day in the life of the city. Their work has
since been adopted by students of the avant-garde and can be read as a
precursor of what came to be known as 'city symphonies', a term that
loosely describes a film of the silent era that is concerned with the city,
its buildings and the way in which the inhabitants interact with it.
They are often characterised by a detached perspective concerning the
human beings who live there. Filmed using long and high-angle shots
and extended pans, people are shown from afar often massed in crowds
and without distinction as individuals.

Although earlier in date than most of the 'city symphonies',
Manhatta certainly fits within the group because of the similarity of its
aesthetic approach. However, we should see it in its original context too,
as it also conforms to a type of film that was common enough at the
time of its release, known as the 'scenic' or 'interest' film.
These subgenres were a staple of cinema shows from the mid-1900s
and were intended to interest a general audience. The 'day in the life'
structure was a common device providing the 'scenic' with some kind
of forward progression and a satisfying beginning and end.
The superimposition on the image of Walt Whitman poems about the
city is again not untypical of films of this period, and there is some
evidence to suggest that the distributor insisted on these to give the
audience some kind of explanatory framework. Short phrases from
various poems[19] are used to comment on the film and bestow a lyrical
quality. *Manhatta* makes particular use of extracts from Whitman's poem
City of Ships in the intertitles:

'City of the world! for all races are here. All the lands of the earth make
contributions here.'

'City of wharves and stores! city of tall façades of marble
and iron!'

The images themselves are spectacular in composition and quality.
The angles chosen are appropriate to the nature of the 'city of tall
façades'; indeed, it is difficult to see New York any other way. From the
opening panorama of the classic skyline seen from the harbour, to the
docking of the ferry as hundreds of workers disgorge on their way to
work, to the roofscapes, it is evident that the film is made with a
photographic artist's eye. Individual shots leave a similar impression on
the viewer as great still images would do – in fact, Strand recreates in
movement his famous still photograph, *Wall Street* (1915). Sheeler, a
painter of the 'precisionist' school, may have selected the supporting
wires of the Brooklyn Bridge, which splay out like a firework, exploding
with perfect symmetry. Our two photographers perch at the top of the
skyscrapers slowly perusing this strange world that resembles a
fantastical landscape of ancient temples. Every now and then as the
steam from the chimneys clears, we manage to catch a glimpse of the
frenetic pace of the city and the human anthill far below.

Dir/Ph: Charles Sheeler, Paul Strand; **Prod Co**: Film Arts Guild.

La Mariée du château maudit
France, 1910 – 12 mins
Albert Capellani

One of the great pleasures of living in the internet age is how it has transformed our ability to make connections which add meaning. This nice little film from a century ago is a case in point. I first saw it at a film festival and admired it for its quality, beautiful locations, lovely colours, trick work and nicely structured supernatural story. I included it in a lecture about the development of the short drama into the feature film, along with Griffith's *Adventures of Dollie**. It wasn't until years later, when I was working on a project about English musical hall, that I stumbled across a song-film (i.e. an early film that had a song to accompany it) with a familiar story. It was based on a traditional song called the 'Mistletoe Bough', known even today by an older generation and in the race memory of folk singers.

The ballad concerns a young bride who, at her wedding celebrations, instigates a game of hide-and-seek. The groom tries to find her, but to no avail. Many years pass and a chest is found by accident; on opening, it is revealed to contain the skeleton of a girl in a bridal gown. A search revealed that this tale was probably introduced into England by the poet Samuel Rogers, who lived in Newington Green, London (where I am writing this now), and where Edgar Allen Poe, connoisseur of premature burial stories, lived for a while. He set the story in Modena, Italy. The song was written down in the 1830s and was traditionally sung standing up 'with solemn chanting' at Christmas gatherings. The telling of Christmas ghost stories continues to this day, now relocated from the fireside or church hall to the cinema and television. There are many other incarnations of this adaptable story – songs, plays and various anecdotal references, such as in Alfred Hitchcock's *Rope* (1948), where it is described as a favourite childhood story of one of the murderers who has concealed his victim in an antique Italian chest.

The Pathé film, then, builds on a shared western culture of such stories and is cleverly positioned as a profit-maximising seasonal offering

for which no expense is spared. It is directed by Albert Capellani, one of
the company's star film-makers, and photographed by another, Segundo
de Chomón, whose photographic trick work was of the highest quality.
They have improved on the story and extracted the best of its visual
potential by shooting on location in a very fine set of actual ruins, which
adds to the gothic feel. The gorgeously dressed wedding guests,
rendered more lovely by expert stencil colouring, organise the game of
hide-and-seek. The bride runs off into the cellars, where she accidentally
locks herself in a room containing a large chest. She opens it to reveal a
skeleton dressed in a bridal gown. An old book lies on a lectern beside
the body and, in a beautifully executed matte shot, little figures appear
on the right and left leaves of the book, telling of the young woman's
fate, the story-within-the-story – the Legend of the Mistletoe Bough.
As she lies trapped in the cellar with the enchanted book, perhaps
destined to share the fate of her predecessor, the bridegroom and
companions search for her in vain until a kitten crawls through the tiny
window of the dungeon alerting them to her location.

Dir: Albert Capellani; **Ph**: Segundo de Chomón.

The Marriage Circle
US, 1924 – 85 mins
Ernst Lubitsch

Hitchcock's favourite Lubitsch film, Lubitsch's favourite Lubitsch film –
what could be better? A *commédie matrimoniale*, or farce, very much in
the Oscar Wilde mould, *The Marriage Circle* was Lubitsch's first proper
Hollywood film and a turning point in the development of his style.
Gone were grand costume dramas such as *Madame Dubarry* (1919) and
the stylised comedies like *The Oyster Princess**, and in came a more adult
and realistic kind of comedy. Like a Wilde play, the plot is extremely
precise and detailed, and would take pages to explain, but essentially it is
set in Vienna ('city of laughter and romance' – that is, with the more
relaxed sexual behaviour of Europe) and concerns two marriages – one
good (Monte Blue and Florence Vidor), one bad (Adolphe Menjou and
Marie Prevost) – and one extra character (Creighton Hale), who is in love
with one of the wives. A series of misunderstandings and backfiring
machinations causes upheaval all round, but is resolved at the end to
everyone's mutual satisfaction.

This type of intricate plot, built on centuries of farce from the
theatre, became one of the most successful film genres of all time, the
romantic comedy. But where Shakespeare and Wilde fashioned their
magic with words, Lubitsch had to work with facial expression. One of
the great legacies of silent cinema is that it produced such accomplished
acting that it hardly needed words. Partly this was achieved by good
direction, in which the actors were given clear instruction on gesture and
facial expression. For example, Adolphe Menjou, in a rare serious
moment in the film, registers a series of expressions that range from
hope, excitement, longing and terrible hurt disappointment when it is
'proved' that his wayward wife is unfaithful. His most memorable
expression, though, occurs when, seeing his wife flirting with another
man, it dawns on him how he can get rid of her for ever, and he lights
up with a smile of pure joy and mischievousness. Likewise, Monte Blue,

when discovered in the arms of a woman by his colleague Gustav, registers terror (at being discovered), relief (when Gustav incorrectly assumes it is his wife), a pretence at male complicity (what can I do? she's crazy about me), as well as signalling Gustav to clear off, all in a few seconds. The techniques of eye-line matching, in which one person's glance guides the viewer to the next person's point of view, condenses the drama, allowing more to be packed into the film, which, along with the clever editing, ensures that the style is purely cinematic despite the theatrical roots of its content. No one has ever accused Lubitsch of being 'stagey'. This gives the whole production a richness and sense of speed – the audience must keep up with the breathless pace, twists and turns, and the delightful frothiness for which Lubitsch's comedies are famous.

Lubitsch set the tone for the development of 'screwball' comedy in the sound era. Famously, Billy Wilder lamented at his funeral, 'No more Lubitsch,' to which William Wyler responded, 'Worse than that – no more Lubitsch films.' To anyone who hasn't seen one, I envy you that first delicious encounter.

Dir: Ernst Lubitsch; **Scr**: Paul Bern, from the play by Lothar Schmidt; **Ph**: Charles Van Enger; **Cast**: Adolphe Menjou, Marie Prevost, Monte Blue, Florence Vidor, Creighton Hale.

Metropolis
Germany, 1927 – 148 mins
Fritz Lang

Now that a complete version of *Metropolis* is finally available thanks to the discovery in 2008 of a near-complete 16mm copy in Argentina, it seems extraordinary that despite missing a fifth of its footage and making no sense, any film should spend over eighty years in the pantheon of iconic silent films. This would seem to indicate that it is *not* plot and pace and elegant narrative continuity that make *Metropolis* great, although it is nice to see them back in the film.

Fritz Lang's masterpiece works on its big ideas and scaled-up vision: an art deco future with gothic undertones. Essentially a parable or moral tale, it foresees a logical conclusion to the processes of industrialisation and urbanisation in a dystopia where society has stratified into the few super-rich, who live in godlike luxury in the highest levels of the vast futurist cityscape, and the masses of exploited and expendable workers, who labour in the lower levels on the great machines that make the city function. These workers have become entirely enslaved by the master of Metropolis, to the point where they have no individuality – they wear uniform clothes, march in miserable, downtrodden step with each other and are known by a number not a name.

The story was written principally by Thea von Harbou, married at this time to Lang, and was original, but with the Russian Revolution still resonating, the themes of futurism and totalitarianism can be traced most directly to Yegeny Zamyatin's *We* (1921), which, along with Jerome K. Jerome's short story 'The New Utopia', and indeed *Metropolis* itself, would directly influence the giants of the dystopia genre, Huxley's *Brave New World* (1931) and Orwell's *Nineteen Eighty-Four* (1949).

However, as is evident, now that we can see the whole film, *Metropolis* is about more than sci-fi. The sections which were cut from the film by the American distributors rounded out the characters: in particular, the motivations of the mad scientist Rotwang and of the master of Metropolis and his relationship with his privileged but sensitive son, Freder. Freder meets Maria, a beautiful preacher who is trying to unite the master and workers, and follows her to the lower levels, where he discovers the true cost to humanity of his luxurious lifestyle. His father cynically engages Rotwang to endow the robot creature he has made for himself with the likeness of Maria. The false Maria, superbly played by the nineteen-year-old Brigitte Helm, is the antithesis of her namesake and whips up the youth of Metropolis into an erotic, murderous frenzy with her exotic dancing. Later, egged on by Rotwang, the robot incites the workers of the lower levels to riot, even to the point of flooding the city and killing their own children. It is Freder who, inspired by his love for the real Maria, becomes a mediator between the master and workers, and together they rescue the children and bring peace to the city – 'between the head and the hands must always be the heart', as the intertitle concludes.

Despite the obvious place its ideas occupy in the annals of science fiction, it is the visual impact of *Metropolis*'s design that leaves the strongest impression and why, even in its abridged form, it has such a cult following. Vast cityscapes with flying machines and overhead railways, architecture built on a scale that dwarfs the individual and, notably, the metal android supply an aesthetic of the future other movie-makers have found irresistible ever since (think of *Things to Come* [1936], *Modern Times* [1936], *Blade Runner* [1982], *Minority Report* [2001], *I Robot* [2004]). And underneath the clean, futuristic upper levels lies the German gothic, replete with medieval and biblical symbolism – the vision of the M-Machine as the god Moloch being fed human sacrifices; the parable Maria tells of the Tower of Babel; Rotwang's alchemist laboratory; and the burning at the stake of the robot by the mob. Certainly, no expense was spared – from the incredibly large and elaborate sets, cutting-edge special effects, fantastic technicians and cast of thousands – it was one of the most expensive productions ever undertaken at that time and a box-office disaster of magnificent proportions.

Dir: Fritz Lang; **Scr**: Thea von Harbou, Fritz Lang; **Ph**: Karl Freunde, Günter Rittau, Walter Ruttmann; **Art Dir**: Otto Hunte, Erich Kettelhut, Karl Vollbrecht; **Cast**: Brigitte Helm, Alfred Abel, Gustav Fröhlich, Rudolf Klein-Rogge.

Monte Cristo
France, 1929 – 223 mins
Henri Fescourt

It is easy to justify the place of individual artists of vision in any list. It is less easy to find space for those who subordinate their film-making skill to the service of their subject, but many very good films are made in this fashion and Henri Fescourt's *Monte Cristo* is a very good film. The plain, realistic style of film-making, anticipating classic Hollywood style, is admirably suited to this adaptation of Alexander Dumas and Auguste Maquet's *The Count of Monte Cristo*. The novel, originally serialised and running at a massive 1,312 pages, is the work of art here and needs no further embellishment from the film-maker. Unlike Abel Gance's approach in *Napoleon*, in which the film itself was the artwork, Henri Fescourt saw his job as retelling this great story in images with the minimum of film-making stylistics on show. One could argue that it is the very lack of recognisably 'artistic' flourishes that makes this film great.

The story, of course, is a classic for a reason. A tale of romance, terrible injustice and revenge, it takes place in a series of gorgeous locations – the Mediterranean, the Middle East, Paris, Marseilles and the terrifying Chateau d'If, where the hero Edmund Dantés is incarcerated by a corrupt official. Fescourt pared down the story to the essentials of the narrative, losing a number of subplots and conflating some elements of the story – in particular, creating a clever new backstory for the characters of Caderousse and Benedetto which saves the audience from a good deal of tedious exposition. This simplification, no doubt infuriating to Dumas purists, allows Fescourt to pace this 4-hour super-production, affording him the luxury of time to present certain scenes in great detail and to develop the characters. This gives a film that could have been ponderous and confusing a lightness reminiscent of a good television drama series.

The scene on the small island of Monte Cristo is a good example. Dantés, having escaped from his prison in the Chateau d'If, is searching for the treasure of his fellow prisoner, the Abbé Faria, but still suspects that it was just the ravings of a mad old man. Following his rough map, he tries several cave entrances – we see him enter one cave and leave again, even though this might be considered a waste of screen time. He surveys the cliffs in a sequence of shot/reverse shots, the camera closing in on him with each movement till his face is in full close-up and we can see the doubt and anticipation in his expression. This allows us to travel alongside him, as it were, experiencing the excitement of the discovery, the labour involved in digging the treasure up and savouring the implications for Dantés's life to come. Added to this, the elegance and orchestration of the film-making is extraordinary. Fescourt used four cameramen to maximise movement, rhythm and to get the best from the locations, many of which are real places from the story. He shot in the Chateau d'If itself and the surrounding islands, filmed authentic old sailing ships coming into Marseilles and, for the interiors, had the talents of the best art director and costume designer in the world at that time, Boris Bilinsky. The scenes at the Paris Opéra and the ball at Monte Cristo's palace are staggeringly opulent. To create such a long movie that is completely immersive and that, as the viewer, you wish would never end is an achievement of the highest order.

Dir/Scr: Henri Fescourt; **Ph**: Henri Barreyre, Maurice Hennebains, Gustavo Kottula, Julien Ringel; **Art Dir/Costumes**: Boris Bilinsky; **Cast**: Jean Angelo, Lil Dagover, Gaston Modot, Jean Toulout, Henri Debain, Robert Mérin, Bernhard Goetzke, Pierre Batcheff.

Nanook of the North: A Story of Life and Love in the Actual Arctic
US, 1922 – 79 mins
Robert J. Flaherty

Quite a few history books cite *Nanook of the North* as the first feature-length documentary, or non-fiction film if they are being very precise. While this is not the case, it doesn't really matter – what is significant about the film is that it captured the zeitgeist when it was released, was widely seen and has consequently been much viewed and written about ever since. So much so, in fact, that it is now a kind of touchstone for debates about the nature of documentary. Often defined by John Grierson's famous description 'the creative treatment of reality', which would certainly describe *Nanook*, 'documentary' is rarely defined by its duration. The significance of its feature-film length is, of course, that it fitted into the exhibition framework of the commercial cinema and was therefore given the kind of attention usually reserved for big fiction productions. It was a commercial success and opened the door to other major non-fiction films such as *The Great White Silence**, *Grass* (1925), *Turksib* (1929) and others.

Another common misconception about *Nanook* is that it is an ethnographic film. Flaherty was not an anthropologist and his motivation for making the film was very clear. He had travelled extensively in the Canadian Arctic, first as a prospector, and had already shot some film on his journeys with Eskimo guides:

> As a part of my exploration equipment, on these expeditions, a motion-picture outfit was included. It was hoped to secure films of the North and Eskimo life, which might prove to be of enough value to help in some way to defray some of the costs of the explorations.[20]

Since the 1900s, no self-respecting expedition travelled without a camera, but Flaherty's first films were not a great success. He admitted as much, attributing the problem to a lack of narrative thread; but inspired by Martin E. Johnson's success with his film *Among the Cannibal Islands of the South Pacific* (1918), and after some years fund-raising, Flaherty managed to get a French fur company, Révillon Frères, to sponsor him to go north again, this time with the sole purpose of shooting a film.

He set up camp in one of the company's trading posts in Inukjuak, Hudson's Bay, and spent a year filming the daily life of an Inuit family as they struggled to survive in an almost inconceivably harsh environment. He selected a hunter called Allakariallak, whom he dubbed 'Nanook', and manufactured a family for him. The family were seen kayaking, fishing, playing, trading furs, building an igloo and sledging with their ferocious huskies. Flaherty filmed Nanook and his companions in various hunting scenes (deprived of their guns, which he felt didn't lend the right air of authenticity) – catching salmon through ice holes, killing walrus, snow fox and seal using the traditional spears and harpoons of the Inuit.

An element of drama is introduced at the end when the family is nearly caught out by an oncoming storm and is forced to shelter in an unused igloo. The film ends with them snug in their icy dome, huddled naked under the bear skins, although the cuteness is kept at bay by a previous comment that the inside of the igloo must be kept below freezing or it will melt. Even if staged, this must have been a hard life. Flaherty's wife, Frances, justified criticism of the film by saying that he was 'building a story from the materials of life', which could cover a host of sins we wouldn't subscribe to in today's ethically scrutinised documentaries. While perhaps overly romanticised for the modern audience, it is still a beautiful film that makes you want to know more and ask questions – another purpose of the documentary.

Dir: Robert J. Flaherty.

Napoleon (Napoléon vu par Abel Gance)
France, 1927 – 332 mins
Abel Gance

It is futile to try and sum up *Napoleon* in the space allotted here; it's far
too big in every way – big man, big subject, big director, big, big film.
It's long, nearly six hours at its latest restored length, and it's lavish, using
all of the tricks and techniques of French Impressionist film-making to
pack a huge emotional wallop, that once seen properly, at full length
with orchestral score and the final triptych (widescreen) ending, is almost
overwhelming. It takes all day to watch, and its length seems to have
dogged the film's distribution since it was made – but how perfect now
for our 'box set' culture. If we can wade through the treacle of
Napoleon's tortuous production history, lack of distribution and the epic
work of reconstruction and restoration, we may get to this magnificent
film. This story, though, is well worth the telling and I can recommend
Kevin Brownlow's book on the film,[21] which is not only a good read but

also an education in the incredible complexities of bringing a creative
vision to an audience through the medium of film.

Originally conceived by director Abel Gance, a man with the
imagination and ambition of a von Stroheim or a Welles, this was to be the
first episode of a six-part life of Napoleon. Despite its length, the film only
gets as far as Napoleon's Italian campaign when he was just twenty-six.
But what an ending! So much better than a biopic, with its inherently
depressing conclusion. There is young Napoleon, poised like an eagle
above Piedmont, about to release his ravenous army onto its fertile plains
below, and from there, to conquer all Europe. The triptych ending –
composed of three full-size images side by side – with its jaw-dropping
scope, brings together the overall imagery of the film, which, despite all
the clever film-making innovations and stylistic devices, is simple and
coherent: Napoleon himself, iconic in the bicorn hat and beautifully
rendered by Albert Dieudonné; the eagle, which is the symbol of his
imperious and independent nature; and the interior mechanics of his mind
represented by mathematical figures, plans, maps and timepieces as he

calculates his line of attack to an infinitesimal degree. (The triptych too is suggestive aesthetically of Napoleon's point of view, with the three parts of his army facing an enemy, choosing between the flanking manoeuvre or the centre position strategy.)

It is clear from the outset that Gance knows Napoleon in obsessive detail, so there are no compromises with historical accuracy, and time (evidently) is spent on the minutiae. His Corsican adventures, the siege of Toulon, the vicissitudes of the Revolutionary Convention, the Terror, the defence of Paris and his wooing of Josephine are given as much space as they need, but for Gance and his generation, art was not so much about truth or authenticity but about creating experience and this is truly 'event' cinema. All of this detail and time, all of the techniques, some learned but many specially created, serve the vision. To name a few: polyvision, multiple superimposition, widescreen lenses, hand-held cameras, night-time filming, light diffusion, mobile cameras, the juxtaposition of scenes (such as the double storm in which a riot breaks out in the Convention as Napoleon is tossed on the waves of a storm at sea), fast editing, rhythmic editing, all kinds of camera angles, vignetting and framing devices, the triptych (a three-camera system not used again till Cinerama and CinemaScope[22]), with its tricolour tinting. Gance even filmed the final reel in 3-D and colour, but found that it was *too* jarring, *too* gimmicky. It was too important, at the end of the film, not to interfere with the audiences' experience of the character. This ultimately was what Gance was after, as Brownlow, who has made his life's work the restoration of this film, confirms: 'Gance did not enlarge the screen simply to stun the audience with a larger picture. As well as gigantic panoramas, Gance split the screen into three, into one central action and two framing actions. In this way he orchestrated the cinema.'

Dir/Scr: Abel Gance; **Ph**: Léonce-Henri Burel, Alexandre Volkoff, Jules Krüger, *et al*.; **Art Dir**: Alexandre Benois; **Cast**: Vladimir Roudenko, Albert Dieudonné, Gina Manès, Nicolas Koline.

(*Previous page*) Abel Gance's vision matches Napoleon's in scale in this stunning triptych finale

The Nibelungen Saga (*Die Nibelungen Saga*)
Germany, 1924 – 291 mins
Fritz Lang

As I mentioned in the introduction, silent film in performance has a sympathy with that other hybrid art form – opera. Nowhere is this more apparent than in Fritz Lang's magnificent *The Nibelungen Saga*. It comes as two films – *Siegfried* and *Kriemhild's Revenge*. Both are over two hours long and although they work as stand-alone films, they are especially powerful seen together. Based on the national German epic, first written down in the twelfth century, its themes not are unlike those of the Arthurian legends, with their codes of kinship and loyalty, and mix of real places and people, set amid fantastical landscapes populated by mythical creatures. Fritz Lang's films are not based in any way on the Wagner *Ring* cycle – in fact, he was keen to treat them differently – but they share the same grand operatic scope, creating one of the most beautiful and unexpectedly emotional films of the silent cinema.

Like all such sagas or song cycles, the action is episodic, here divided into 'cantos', which perfectly suits the Expressionist film-making style – it is all about composition, moving from set-up to set-up, shot head-on to take in the panoramic landscape or moving in to close-ups of the characters. The sets, built with no expense spared at the Ufa Neubabelsberg studio, are massive, with vast oversized forests and glades, frozen rivers, underground caverns and castles. The interiors are sparsely furnished, the solid architecture framing the action, but we get no feeling of an outside world – there are few ordinary people, and no towns or villages. As the hero Siegfried travels from his forest smithy to the Burgundian court, he passes alone through these fantastical, oversized landscapes, encountering the dragon and the king of the dwarfs, from whom he takes possession of the cloak of invisibility and the great Nibelungen hoard which will seal his fate.

The sets are integrated with the design of the décor and costumes, displaying abstract patterns and sharp contrasts of light and dark.

These are coded so that Kriemhild, who will become Siegfried's wife, is first dressed in white; on the death of Siegfried, she is dressed in black signifying her grief and desire for revenge. There is also a marked contrast between the two films. In the first, the scheme is clean, bright and angular; the second is dark, asymmetrical and organic. Siegfried, Kriemhild's first love, is fair, straight-limbed and young, where Attila, her second husband, whom she weds only to pursue vengeance, is old, grotesque and misshapen.

There is an equally marked contrast between the two films in terms of the narrative: the first part starts as an optimistic tale of a young hero in search of fortune and love, while the second is the tragic tale of a grief-stricken woman bent on revenge. As in all sagas of the Middle Ages, the story is driven by the complex web of oaths and personal loyalties that pervade the court – not unlike gangster narratives of more recent years, with their potential for fatalism and tragedy. Innocent individuals are caught in impossible moral situations, so that, despite the grand scale, the film is also made up of some extremely moving, intimate moments. The stately pace emphasises the control of the acting, particularly that of Kriemhild, played with great dignity by Margarethe Schön, who must convey in long takes, almost without moving, a seething battle of emotions. The music is integral to this, the massive romantic score by Gottfried Huppertz affording emotional depth, colour and drama. As in opera, the music is half of the production and, without being too purist, I would recommend that you see both films as a whole work complete with their original musical score.

Dir: Fritz Lang; **Scr**: Thea von Harbou; **Ph**: Carl Hoffman, Günther Rittau; **Art Dir**: Otto Hunte, Erich Kettelhut, Karl Vollbrecht; **Music**: Gottfried Huppertz; **Cast**: Paul Richter, Margarethe Schön, Hanna Ralph, Theodor Loos, Hans Aldalbert Schlettow, Rudolf Rittner, Rudolf Klein-Rogge.

(*Opposite page*) Only a story as ambitious as the Nibelungen saga could justify the huge sets built at the Ufa studio

Nosferatu: A Symphony of Horrors (*Nosferatu: Eine Symphonie des Grauens*)
Germany, 1922 – 89 mins
F. W. Murnau

The really good horror films don't just scare us – they haunt us.
Death, disease, contagion, blood, rot, rats, the damp earth of the
graveyard and the horrors of the night are all ingredients of the vampire
story and still have the power to chill at 3 o'clock in the morning, 'the
soul's midnight'. F. W. Murnau's *Nosferatu* is subtitled 'a symphony of
horrors' and it uses every cinematic instrument to instil a sense of unease
and growing dread in the audience. Vampire lore has since become so
sophisticated that we almost have to remind ourselves that it is not real.
It is becoming difficult to imagine a time when there was a film-maker
who hadn't seen a vampire film, so closely has the monster come to be
identified with the particular medium of cinema. But there was a first,
and this is it. The original and best, and the model for all vampire films
to come.

Everyone has their favourite moment from this film – the image of
Nosferatu's shadow on the wall as he climbs the stairs is probably the
most iconic. For me, the best moments in the film are the little Murnau
touches: the speeded-up carriage, which is so 'wrong' now in terms of
film grammar but suggests some horrific scuttling insect; or that moment
when the deserted ship arrives in the town and the hatchway opens on a
well of darkness below – we look, knowing perfectly well what will
happen, but Murnau leaves it a couple of heartbeats longer than
expected, so that when the vampire emerges, it makes us jump.
What reminds me most of the later grammar of horror film is a sequence
of shots that occurs just after that famous shadow has appeared. We see
Ellen (the Mina character, married to Hutter, for which read Jonathan
Harker) clutching her heart in anguish as she senses the vampire
approaching. As she backs away, we can only see her face as the
monster comes closer, until the shadow of that horrible hand hovers over

Still the scariest vampire film of all

her heart and suddenly clenches, causing her to gasp with pain. In an immediate match cut, Hutter clutches the professor's dressing gown, over his heart, and violently shakes him awake. This little shock seems very modern for a film of 1922.

Why is it still the best? The Coppola version of 1992 is a more authentic interpretation of the book, the Hammer Dracula films are sexier, the Anne Rice vampire adaptations and later refinements are more in tune with the times; so why should a 1922 silent film retain such a long-lasting influence and continue to appeal to each generation? I think it is the *Mitteleuropa*-gothic-Germanness that brings the medieval back into the present and still taps into our primal fears of the elemental and the bestial. The designer, Albin Grau, whose idea it was to adapt Bram Stoker's story and whom Christopher Frayling describes as, aside from Murnau, 'the most important creative intelligence'[23] on *Nosferatu*, designed every aspect of the film to evoke that period but without conflicting with its nineteenth-century setting. The fusion of German Romantic art and the gothic is called to mind by the woodcut titles and poster artwork, the use of real locations, and the make-up and costume of Max Schreck, with his elongated fingers and nails, bats' ears and needle-like buck teeth. Henrik Galeen, the screenwriter, chose to equate vampirism with plague and rats, further invoking the Middle Ages.

In fact, fear of contagion suffuses the film, and it is often assumed that this is a reference to the flu epidemic of 1918/19, but could just as likely reflect a contemporary concern about the rampant increase of venereal disease after World War I, when returning men infected their wives and an increasingly sexualised female population probably infected them right back. The film finally finds us a more romantic cure for the vampire, who can only be destroyed by the sacrificed blood of a woman 'without sin' and the return of the light.

Dir: F. W. Murnau; **Scr**: Henrik Galeen; **Ph**: Fritz Arno Wagner; **Art Dir**: Albin Grau; **Cast**: Max Schreck, Alexander Granach, Greta Schroeder, Gustav von Wangenheim.

The Oyster Princess (*Die Austernprinzessin*)
Germany, 1919 – 60 mins
Ernst Lubitsch

Like most great comedians, Ernst Lubitsch was profoundly subversive while apparently pleasing everybody. And though the legendary 'Lubitsch touch' is difficult to explain, after one or two exposures you begin to recognise it when you watch one of his comedies. Those who know, see it, those who don't, think it is just general silliness, but Lubitsch always manages to sneak past some naughty adult stuff.

This early feature-length comedy was a star vehicle for Ossi Oswalda and although very much part of the mainstream of commercial cinema, it is distinctly counterculture in feel. Described as a 'grotesk Lustspiel' (grotesque comedy doesn't quite translate that lovely phrase), the film concerns an American billionaire oyster tycoon (Victor Janson), who is waited on hand and foot by an army of servants, and his spoilt brat of a daughter (Oswalda). After one of Oswalda's friends marries a count, she throws a tantrum and trashes the house, momentarily calming down when her father promises to procure her a prince, before trashing the house out of sheer joy. A matchmaker sets her up with a penniless prince (Harry Liedtke), but he sends his friend Josef (Julius Falkenstein) to check her out, leading to inevitable confusion when Josef is mistaken for the prince himself. The Oyster Princess, although concerned that Josef looks a bit stupid, drags him off to the priest to be married instantly (quite literally – the priest marries them through the open window on which she has tapped). There follows the wedding feast, during which Josef, who hasn't eaten for a while, stuffs himself, while ranks of servants serve the guests in choreographed manoeuvres, like a well-oiled machine. An 'epidemic' of the foxtrot breaks out, and everyone dances the night away.

After the guests have gone, the Oyster Princess goes to bed, firmly ejecting the new husband from her room. She is considerably more enthusiastic about the real prince, however, when she encounters him by chance the next day at a meeting of the 'Billionaires Daughters Society for Combating Dipsomania'. He is brought in horribly drunk, but an instant physical rapport leads her to box for him, winning him from the other ladies in a fair fight. She takes him home and with little compunction deposits him in her bedroom. They kiss and, after a moment's anguish that they will be parted for ever by her marriage, discover that Josef has wed her in the Prince's name, and so a second wedding dinner takes place, this time with only the father in attendance. They can't keep their hands off each other and soon rush off to the bedroom, which in a film culture where sex was rigorously normative strikes an odd note, but there is much to enjoy in this risqué undermining of the institution of marriage.

None of this really explains the unusualness of the film, or the comedy, which lies in small witty details that are somehow integral to the narrative. It is most similar perhaps to the microcosmic observational humour of Jane Austen, but set in a visual framework that carries equal weight with the characterisation – the design is glorious. This thoroughly modern type of self-reliant heroine goes on to become a staple of classical Hollywood comedy largely through Lubitsch's direct influence, although the delicious naughtiness is submerged after the imposition of the Hays Code.

Dir: Ernst Lubitsch; **Scr**: Hanns Kräly, Ernst Lubitsch; **Tech Dir**: Kurt Waschneck; **Ph**: Theodor Sparkul; **Art Dir**: Kurt Richter; **Cast**: Victor Janson, Ossi Oswalda, Harry Liedtke, Julius Falkenstein.

Page of Madness (*Kurutta ippeiji*)
Japan, 1926 – 60 mins
Teinosuke Kinugasa

Confusion is the watchword for Kinugasa's masterpiece of silent
Japanese cinema, not only in its subject matter, which explores the
borders between memory, nightmares and insanity, but also for the
incomplete version of this film that has come down to us through the
decades. If you have seen the 60-minute version of this film – most likely
in the context of 1920s avant-garde art – and came away bewildered,
then you are in good company. If you haven't seen it, it is helpful to
know that the film is missing up to two reels of footage and lacks the
commentary that in Japan would have been delivered by a *benshi*,
a narrator who would explain the characters and action of the film to the
audience. In fact, a written *benshi* commentary does survive for a part of
the film, which might shed light on a story that is difficult to understand
at first viewing.

From what we can gather, the film concerns a man (we see him once
in a naval uniform) who has taken a job as a janitor in an asylum so that
he can look after his insane wife. Much of the film takes place within the
asylum in a series of flashbacks, visions, memories or nightmares.
The janitor (played with almost unbearable pathos by Masuo Inoue) is
visited by a younger female character, who, we can work out later, must
be the couple's daughter; she appears in various scenes with a young
man to whom she has become engaged, then married, which seems to
be a cause of conflict. There are also confused images of an infant and
something being thrown into water, which may indicate the cause of the
wife's insanity and incarceration. The ambiguity of the images, created in
rhythmic montage, distortion and superimposition, and the lack of
elucidation give rise to dreadful imaginings. Interesting, too, is the fact
that the nightmare of insanity seems not to be connected to the asylum
itself. This is no Bedlam. In fact, the institution seems to be relatively
enlightened, with sympathetic doctors and a routine that incorporates

beautiful gardens in which the patients can roam at will. Other inmates exhibit extreme insanity, justifying their confinement: in particular, a violent male patient and a young girl who dances incessantly, both of whom become catalysts for riotous outbreaks by the inmates.

Although the image of bars is repeated constantly, often sweeping across the image from side to side, it is the prison of the mind that Kinugasa concentrates on, not the institution as prison.

In his desperation to help his suffering wife, the janitor tries to free her one night, but she becomes hysterical as he shows her the door leading outside. Of her own volition, she returns to her cell and to the catatonic state in which she has chosen to reside. All he can do is to stay close and present to her a vision of her potential wellness in a delightful scene where he distributes cheerful-faced Noh masks to the inmates and everyone is smiling and laughing. This occasional foray into optimistic imagery, represented by a field of flowers or the sparkling lights of the fair, makes the bareness of the cell and barrenness of the mind more starkly tragic.

Even with the lack of commentary and the missing scenes, *A Page of Madness* is a traumatic, powerful and self-consciously constructed film and presents one of the most successful attempts, in the silent or any era, to visualise the inner thoughts of the mind in film.

Dir/Prod: Teinosuke Kinugasa; **Scr**: Yasunari Kawabata; **Ph**: Kohei Sugiyama; **Art Dir**: Chiyo Ozaki; **Cast**: Masuo Inoue, Yoshie Nakagawa, Ayako Iijima, Eiko Minami, Hiroshi Nemoto.

Pandora's Box (*Die Büchse der Pandora*)
Germany, 1928 – 133 mins
G. W. Pabst

The reputation of *Pandora's Box* has continued to grow since its release in the heyday of Weimar Germany. This is partly due to the timeless icon that is Louise Brooks, but also because of Frank Wedekind's two groundbreaking plays on which the film was based, the exquisite elegance of the film-making by director Georg Wilhelm Pabst and the eternally popular appeal of 'Jack the Ripper' stories.

The image of Louise Brooks is probably better known now than when the film was released, reproduced as it has been down the years, particularly in still photography. The face so symmetrical with its razor-sharp bob haircut, reminiscent of a cartoon, is perfect. This is not to undermine the achievement of Brooks the actress, who gives an extremely fine performance as Lulu, a consummate actress herself and showgirl-cum-professional mistress who exerts an irresistible pull on all around her. She is easygoing, childlike, generous, light-footed and carelessly amoral, well aware of her effect on men but without guilt. Later reviews sometimes refer to her as 'nymphomanic' or a victim of her own desires, but this is not borne out by the film itself and rather proves the playwright's point (Wedekind, a most interesting creative force, was ahead of his time about bourgeois hypocrisy in sexual matters). Lulu is quite capable of cynically throwing a tantrum in order to keep her wealthy patron in line, which she does in a fantastically breathless set piece, keeping an entire theatre waiting (and us) for her to appear on stage. She is puzzled by the lesbian Countess who is in love with her, and uses her shamelessly, but maternal to her former lover's son. At the other end of her fatal and fatalistic downward trajectory, when she is reduced to prostitution in London (strangely Victorian-looking but appropriate for the time the play was written), she encounters the 'Ripper' character and, he being penniless, offers herself to him for free.

Louise Brooks as Lulu accepts the comfort of the wrong stranger

The career of G. W. Pabst has undergone some reassessment
recently, and a simple analysis of the structure of *Pandora's Box* as well
as the editing gives the lie to the suggestion that he was only as good
as his material. Perhaps unnoticed by the modern audience, it is more
about quality than novelty – the continuity editing is flawless and the
establishment of pace, mood and style for each Act or episode is
masterly. It is a dark film – literally and figuratively – but not in the

style of Expressionism; this is social realism, a film of the *Neue Sachlichkeit* or 'new objectivity' which characterised many German films of the later 1920s, and yet its themes of sex, money and death may seem the stuff of melodrama. It is a film that bears repeated viewing and obsessive scrutiny.

Dir: G. W. Pabst; **Scr**: Ladislaus Vajda, based on two plays by Frank Wedekind; **Ph**: Günther Krampf; **Cast**: Louise Brooks, Fritz Kortner, Francis Lederer, Alice Roberts, Gustav Diessl.

Panorama du Grand Canal vu d'un bateau
France, 1896 – 1 min
Auguste and Louis Lumière

The story goes that Alexandre Promio, a young(ish) man sent out into the world by the Lumière brothers in 1896 (their first full year of production) to take views of famous places and people, was apologetic about this first effort. He had mounted his camera in a boat and photographed the palaces of the Grand Canal, creating the first film 'panorama'. Promio's account doesn't quite make sense, as the move was inspired, providing not only the essential movement that was part of the attraction of the Cinématographe but also delivering views of these desirable locations in greater quality than had been possible before. It was the first of hundreds if not thousands of similar views. The panorama was already a familiar concept in other media – including illustrations, maps and plans, stereoscopes, the great panopticons, vast city-centre panorama shows of the early nineteenth century – but the moving pictures brought a fresh dimension to the form and one that still succeeds on its own merits today. The films are as pleasurable now as they were then; a view is a view whether one wants to see it because it is exotic or historic.

Now we can see Venice as it looked over a hundred years ago (actually no different), or London or Paris. Promio took beautiful panoramic shots of the Houses of Parliament along the Thames in 1897 and filmed the ornate pavilions of the International Exhibition of 1900 from the Seine as it arcs round the base of the Eiffel Tower. British pioneer Cecil Hepworth captured similar spectacular views at the same event, while the cameraman from the American company Edison took a whole series of views – horizontal views from boats, vertical views from the elevators in the Eiffel Tower and forward-travelling shots of the moving walkway, which was one of the attractions at the exhibition. These travelling shots were technically known as 'phantom rides' and could be taken from the front of a train or tram, later the motorcar, on roller coasters and merry-go-rounds, and gave the sensation of movement that proved so addictive to audiences. Soon new movements would be added as cameras were designed that could swivel and tilt, but mounting the camera on a moving object is still very much a pleasure of the film, and internet sites seem perfectly suited to sharing these moving views – the short film and panoramic views have never been so popular.

Dir: Lumière brothers; **Ph**: Alexandre Promio.

Paris qui dort (*The Crazy Ray*)
France, 1925 – 34 mins
René Clair

In 1923, the young René Clair was given a brief to film a short comedy using cast and crew who were hanging round the studio on contract waiting for the final part of a serial to be greenlit: surely every first-time director's dream – a competent, talented team and the whole of Paris to play in. The plot was apparently dreamed up in a haze of opium fumes, but it is not so much mystical as a youthful 'what if …?'; nowadays, however, it is most often mentioned in the context of science fiction, and, indeed, the opening of the film finds us (as cinema viewers eighty-five years on) in strangely familiar territory.[24]

A young man wakes to find he is alone in the middle of a city. He is the nightwatchman (Albert) on the iconic Eiffel Tower. He descends from his iron eyrie to the eerier deserted streets of Paris, wandering alone along the boulevards and occasionally encountering figures frozen in mid-action. He comes across one who is apparently about to jump into the Seine, but the man is motionless. Albert, seeing a suicide note, makes an intervention by stuffing money in the man's hand so he will see it if he wakes. He soon meets the only other 'alive' people in Paris, who have been spared this fate because they were in an airplane at the time of the phenomenon. They soon begin to take advantage of the situation and wander over the city doing all the things you can't do normally – drink champagne for free, steal people's clothes and pearls, swim in the city's fountains and picnic on the Eiffel Tower, surveying their kingdom spread out below. The fantasy of having the entire city at your disposal has a strong appeal and is one that recurs frequently in cinema. The fantasy is made yet more appealing by Clair's ability to get air round the subject – his imagery of the young lovers, like angels in beautiful white clothes, perched high above the city on the edge of the lattice of ironwork, is a moment apart – it steals time.

Human nature being what it is, this heavenly state of affairs cannot last – ennui sets in – for what good are these riches? The men fight over

Suspended animation – lovers picnic as the city sleeps

the one girl, and anxiety about the permanence of the situation begins to trouble them. They come down to earth with a bump when it transpires that a mad scientist has put the world to sleep with a 'crazy ray' that can be reversed. As the world springs to life again, there is a moment of real regret that the holiday is over and the rules of the game are reasserted. The lovers wander the streets but are unable to do anything, even sit down, without spending money they don't have. The oppressiveness is too much. A brief excursion back to the lab to freeze the city once more and pick up the much-needed cash doesn't turn out well – the morality of the world, turned briefly upside down, is here to stay and they must make the best of it.

Dir: René Clair; **Ph**: Maurice Desfassiaux, Alfred Guichard; **Art Dir**: André Foy; **Cast**: Henri Rollan, Albert Préjean, Charles Martinelli, Madeleine Rodrigue, Louis Pré fils, Myla Seller, Marcel Vallée, Antoine Stacquet.

The Passion of Joan of Arc (La Passion de Jeanne d'Arc)
France, 1928 – 110 mins
Carl Theodor Dreyer

Of all the film versions of the story of Joan of Arc, this is the one that haunts the viewer with the sense of having witnessed something personally, despite its extreme stylisation. The clue to Dreyer's intention is in the title, *The 'Passion' of Joan of Arc*: the film focuses on the suffering and death of the character of Jeanne in imitation of the Passion of Christ. It is intended not as a 'life' or heroic story but as a documentary (Dreyer used the actual word) based on a remarkable survival, the original transcript of Jeanne's trial from 1431. Dreyer wants the audience to witness that process to the exclusion of all extraneous detail of her life and her actions, save what transpires in the course of her interrogation. The film concentrates on the theological issues, for although Jeanne might have been accused of secular crimes by the English authorities, against whom she had so successfully fought, the issue of most concern to the ecclesiastical court that tried her was her insistence that she would not reveal or discuss her revelations from God (the voices that were her inspiration), thus severely undermining the authority of the Church. She was eventually burned at the stake as a lapsed heretic, having signed an abjuration under threat of torture, which she later recanted.

Having limited himself to this modest slice of the unprecedented amount of information we have about this medieval teenager, Jeanne d'Arc, Dreyer brought all of his considerable skill to creating a visual style that would reveal some kind of truth not bound by storytelling convention. For this reason, he eschewed continuity editing in order to keep the audience unsettled, using, with the help of cameraman Rudolph Maté, unusual off-centre framing and low angles, 'crossing the line'[25] and even shots taken upside down. This creates a sense of disorientation and close involvement with the actors, who are very exposed in big close-up and with no make-up. The sets by Hermann Warm (who also worked on *The Cabinet of Dr. Caligari**) are plain but irregular, with intense white backgrounds that throw the faces of the actors into sharp relief. The shots are dominated by close-ups, particularly of Renée Falconetti who plays Jeanne, in one of the best performances yet recorded on film. There are no establishing shots, which contributes to the sense of disorientation and empathy with Jeanne as she is harangued, mocked (in one scene, just as Christ was mocked) and threatened by leering, angry or sly faces as a series of unnamed judges try to force or trick her into confession.

The final scene is one of the most harrowing in film history, as we are forced to watch the burning itself. In a long shot, Jeanne is tied to the stake having had the comfort of the crucifix taken away from her – she drops the rope and automatically, being helpful, picks it up and hands it to the executioner. This little detail is in keeping with the attempt at verisimilitude which Dreyer was trying to create in bringing to life an age in which reportage did not exist, but it also encapsulates the artless nature of this nineteen-year-old peasant girl, who could not be outwitted by the best minds of the medieval Church. The experience is devastating in precisely the same way as watching a documentary.

Dir/Scr: Carl Theodor Dreyer; **Ph**: Rudolph Maté, Joseph Kottula; **Art Dir**: Hermann Warm, Jean Victor Hugo; **Cast**: Renée Falconetti, Eugène Silvain, Antonin Artaud.

People on Sunday (*Menschen am Sonntag*)
Germany, 1930 – 74 mins
Robert Siodmak, Edgar Ulmer, Rochus Gleise

People on Sunday is an astonishing work of cinematic realism. Or is it neorealism? In its use of real locations, virtual real time and non-professional actors, its tendency to focus on working-class characters coping with modern life and a downplaying of plot, it could be seen as a precursor of the neorealist films of the 1940s. Equally, we can see elements of *People on Sunday* in earlier films of the 1920s, most directly in *Rien que les heures* (1926) and *Berlin: Symphony of a City**. It adopts the same structure of 'a day in the life of' but, instead of focusing on the city itself, chooses to extract one story (among the four million of Berlin) of a set of its citizens, on a glorious summer's Sunday – all stunningly photographed by Eugen Schüfftan.

As the opening titles state, it was based on 'a reportage', or anecdote, of Kurt Siodmak, which accurately reflects the way the story is told, with all its minutiae. As Siodmak put it in a later interview,[26] his initial idea was: boy meets girl in the city and arranges to go the Wannsee on Sunday; he brings his best friend, she brings her (prettier) friend and first boy goes after second girl – a simple idea. It was to be filmed in actual locations using real Berliners to play the five young protagonists (the 'best friend' has a young wife at home who chooses to spend her entire Sunday in bed, so we only see her at the beginning and end of the day). It is important to mention the origins of the core narrative of the film, as writers often lose sight of this in their keenness to attribute this or that factor to one of its film-makers, a starry group of youngsters who went on to become Hollywood directors. But it is this core narrative that reveals how acute the film-makers' observation is.

In the key scene, the single male, who we have already established is a womaniser, is chasing both girls through the woods; the girls split and you expect to see him stop and make a choice, but he does not hesitate in his pursuit of Girl Two. He catches up, she eludes him, he stops chasing, so she stops running; there is a point when he seems to be forcing the situation and she resists, but then she gives in to the moment and we assume sex ensues as the camera pans away through the trees to alight momentarily on a pile of rusty cans and then back to the post-coital couple. This is presented with no particular moral overtone – it is what young people do on a summer's day. If the pile of rubbish holds any significance, it is perhaps a meditation on the temporary nature of such encounters – anti-romantic but not judgmental. The young man is (of course) immediately irritated by her, as she (inevitably) construes the event as evidence of his interest, the prelude to a relationship. He spends the rest of the afternoon trying to shake her off. It is very modern. If you put the actors in jeans and gave them mobile phones and iPods, they would behave in exactly the same way today.

The historical perspective is neither here nor there, however – the essential importance of the film is its ability to strike a chord with audiences as much now as then, for we are all young once.
The precise details that make up the young Berliners' day out – the looks and glances mostly conveyed in close-up – reveal the expectations and pleasures, the disappointments and confusions. They feel very authentic and true, which is timeless film-making genius.

Dir: Robert Siodmak, Edgar Ulmer, Rochus Gleise; **Scr**: Billy Wilder (from an idea by Kurt Siodmak); **Ph**: Eugen Schüfftan, Fred Zinnemann; **Cast**: Erwin Splettstößer, Brigitte Borchert, Cristl Ehlers, Wolfgang von Waltershausen, Annie Schreyer.

The Perils of Pauline
US, 1914 – 180 of 410 mins
Louis Gasnier, Donald MacKenzie

As fiction films became longer in the early teens, a number of different
exhibition strategies based on the more settled and predictable
economics of cinema circuits began to emerge. One strategy was to
produce sequels to exploit successful longer dramas like *The White Slave
Trade** films from Denmark. Another was to make drama series and
serials in which a narrative continued over the course of a longer film
issued in short episodes of one to three reels (20–30 minutes' running
time). Such films could be easily incorporated as special features into the
existing mixed programmes of shorts maintained by many cinemas,
particularly at the more modest end of the industry. These were
supported by lavish marketing campaigns, with billboards, posters,
competitions and serialised print editions in the affiliated press.

　　The Perils of Pauline, made by the American Pathé company in 1914,
was a popular early example starring the twenty-five-year-old Pearl
White, an attractive, athletic actress who played the heiress Pauline with
great energy and delighted audiences with her physical courage.
She performed her own daring stunts, and exhibited an independent
spirit befitting a young lady of the modern age. The victim of a villainous
Secretary (Paul Panzer) left in charge of her fortune, the unsuspecting
Pauline desires nothing more than to go out into the world and
experience enough adventures to inspire a book before settling down
with fiancé, Harry. She gets more than she bargained for, however, as the
Secretary makes repeated attempts on her life, exposing her to
increasingly tricky and dangerous situations from which she must
extricate herself or be rescued by the faithful Harry. These include a series
of daring escapes: from flooded, rat-infested cellars or dilapidated
warehouses involving leaps over cliffs, dives from ocean liners or via
modern contraptions such as hot-air balloons and telegraph wires.
Born of nineteenth-century melodramas, these serials were filled with

sensational features: hooded gangsters from exotic lands, kidnaps and inventive means of torture, chases and last-minute rescues. Episodes were given lurid titles to create a sense of excitement and dread – 'The Goddess of the Far East', 'The Aerial Wire', 'A Tragic Plunge', 'The Reptile under the Flowers' and 'The Floating Coffin'.

As far as we can tell from the surviving fragments, the American serials never quite attained the sophisticated levels of film-making that characterised the best of Feuillade's work for Gaumont in France, but those starring Pearl White were among the best, and with the release of the next series, *The Exploits of Elaine* (known in France as *Les Mystères de New York*), Pearl White became very popular there and all over Europe. Just as well, as the only surviving copies of *The Perils of Pauline* are from 28mm European versions. It's a real shame that only nine episodes of twenty survive, so we may never be able to judge its true qualities.

Dir: Louis Gasnier, Donald MacKenzie; **Scr**: Charles W. Goddard (from his novel), Bertram Millhauser; **Ph**: Arthur C. Miller; **Cast**: Pearl White, Paul Panzer, Crane Wilbur, Donald MacKenzie, Edward José.

The Phantom Carriage (*Körkarlen*)
Sweden, 1921 – 93 mins
Victor Sjöström

Christmas and New Year have traditionally been a time for the fireside
telling of ghost stories and moral tales; a time for contemplation and
assessment of one's life, with the possibility of redemption.
Since Dickens' *A Christmas Carol*, these tales have become a yearly ritual,
so too was Victor Sjöström's film of *The Phantom Carriage*,
a retelling of Selma Lagerlöf's famous story. The film was released on
New Year's Day and became a fixture. Ingmar Bergman used to watch
this film every year, and anyone who has seen *The Seventh Seal* (1957)
will immediately notice the influence of one shot in particular, in which
the robed driver with his scythe makes his way in Death's carriage across
a hilltop, silhouetted against the sky.

This terrifying medieval figure creates an atmosphere of dread
against which the contemporary story is played out. That tale is bleak
enough, starting with a deathbed scene in which a Salvation Army girl,
Edit, dying of consumption, asks for David Holm to be brought to her.
We see David Holm and his drinking companions sitting in the
churchyard just before midnight on New Year's Eve. He tells them a story
about Georges, a friend of his, who relates the legend of the phantom
carriage, according to which the last person to die before midnight on
New Year's Eve must drive the cart to collect the souls of the dead for a
year, each year being like a hundred in life. Holm reveals that Georges'
worst fears have come to pass and he died on New Year's Eve.

Back in the present, one of the Salvation Army officers tells Holm
that Edit is dying and has asked for him, but he drunkenly dismisses him.
His friends try to persuade him and a fight ensues, during which Holm is
impaled on a broken bottle and collapses on a gravestone. In a stunning
scene using in-camera superimposition, the ghostly driver, Georges,
arrives as David's soul rises from his body. Georges tells him that he must
now take over as Death's servant and that his torment will be made

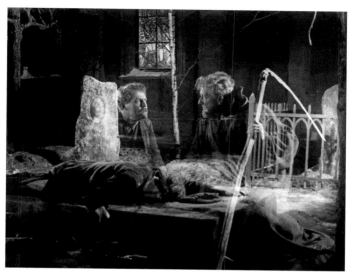

Superimposition represents the supernatural as Death's messenger comes for the soul of David Holm

worse by the sins he committed in life. In a series of flashbacks, he reveals how alcoholism ruined his idyllic life with his wife and two little girls, his imprisonment and cruel treatment of Edit, who tries to help him but becomes infected with TB for her pains. In a terrifying domestic scene, where his wife has locked him in the kitchen to protect the babies from his drunken rage, he breaks down a door with an axe (impossible not to think of *The Shining* [1980] here). Ultimately, he is brought to his senses by the catalogue of his sins at Edit's bedside and at last appeals to God to prevent a future in which his wife poisons herself and their children.

The crafting of *The Phantom Carriage*, as well as the multi-layered story, makes this an unforgettable film. The acting is naturalistic, the characters three-dimensional, and if the use of superimposition to create ghostly apparitions and even the device of the soul coming out of the body were not new (they appear in a British film, *The Little Match Seller*, as early as 1902), the execution of the effects is stunning.

Dir/Scr: Victor Sjöström, from the novel by Selma Lagerlöf; **Ph**: Julius Jaenzon; **Cast**: Victor Sjöström, Astrid Holm, Hilda Borgström, Tore Svennberg.

Policeman (*Keisatsukan*)
Japan, 1933 – 121 mins
Tomu Uchida

Is it anachronistic to think in terms of a silent 'film noir'? This Japanese gangster film predates by eight years the first noir (widely considered to be *The Maltese Falcon* in 1941), but the term conveys the tone, atmosphere and look of this film better than any other. The art of silent film lingered for some years in Japan while the industry caught up with the technological revolution of sound. As a result, a handful of extraordinary films by the great names of Japanese cinema, such as Ozu, Naruse, Uchida and Mizoguchi, were made in the early 1930s, bringing them closer perhaps to the era we associate with the development of the gangster picture in the US. In subject matter also, there is a similarity between this film and the later American productions.

The film concerns two childhood friends from the wrong side of the tracks who choose different paths – one becoming a policeman, the other a villain. In the original stage play of *Keisatsukan*, Tomioka, the villain, was a member of the Communist Party, but for political reasons director Tomu Uchida toned down this aspect in favour of a more conventional gangland setting, and perhaps that is why it feels so familiar to a modern audience used to gangsterdom in all its incarnations and the moral ambiguities that go with the territory. Also resonant is the darkness and fatalism that we associate with film noir. This is apparent from the moment policeman Itami recognises his childhood friend Tomioka waiting at a police checkpoint that has been set up to catch the killer of Itami's friend and mentor. There is an inevitability that Tomioka will be revealed as the killer, but it is the portrayal of their friendship (which, with Uchida's use of sustained close-up, has an almost erotic charge) that lifts the film out of the realms of the police procedural. The conflicts between friendship and professional duty unfold with relentless, impending tragedy, underscored by the gritty imagery of city backstreets and drinking dens. Transfer these elements to the streets of post-World War II Vienna and you have Carol Reed's *The Third Man* (1949). The film ends similarly with a chase, this time over the rooftops, and a climactic shoot-out as Itami is forced to choose between his calling and his friend.

Dir: Tomu Uchida; **Scr**: Eizo Yamuchi, from a story by Toshihiko Takeda; **Ph**: Soichi Aisaka; **Cast**: Isamu Kosugi, Eiji Nakano, Taisuke Matsumoto.

Poor Little Rich Girl
US, 1917 – 65 mins
Maurice Tourneur

Poor Little Rich Girl is a curiously apt title for a Mary Pickford film.
'Poor' only in the sense that she became typecast to the point where,
as a twenty-five-year-old woman, she found herself playing a little girl of
eleven. The 'rich' was real enough, at $10,000 a week. After the success
of this film, she could command any salary she liked. Even the writer,
Frances Marion, who had been writing for Pickford since 1912, was
advanced $50,000 to continue to churn 'em out. They were a good
team, they knew just what the public wanted and supplied it at
eye-watering rates. But although Mary Pickford's name is still current as a
legendary figure in the rise of Hollywood, very few people today have
seen any of her films. Now that some of the films are being restored,
we can at last judge for ourselves why she was so popular with
audiences. Although she was very photogenic, with the looks that
particularly appealed to her generation, her juvenile and later 'little girl'
roles were quite modern, exhibiting precisely the same qualities that we
admire in the heroines of our children's literature today – self-reliance,
with a fierce spirit in defence of others. Early features like *Poor Little Rich
Girl* marked the beginning of Hollywood's long love affair with plots
concerning abused but resourceful orphans.

In the film, Pickford plays a lonely child ignored by rich parents who
are too busy with business or good works. She is minded by jealous and
abusive servants, and allowed no companionship or play. Her over-
exuberance on her occasional contacts with the outside world only
confirm her elders' belief about her wilfulness. As her parents throw a
party for her birthday downstairs, from which she is excluded, the maid
gives the child a double dose of a strong sedative so that she can sneak
out for the night. This induces a dangerous delirium into which the little
girl incorporates all the characters from her daily life in a fantasy forest,
'where things appear as they really are' – the maid, disturbingly, has two

faces which spin round and round – but she also has friends who accompany her on her journey like the scarecrow and the tin man from *The Wizard of Oz* (1939) (these are workmen and servants who have befriended her in real life). Later the journey reaches a crisis point, in which a kindly lady in black drapery offers eternal sleep. This tempts the little girl for a moment, but as she turns from the outstretched hand, she sees beyond it a moonlit graveyard. Back at the dying child's bedside, the doctor tells her mother and father that her 'little journey may be done', but at the last minute in the fantasy world, she is enticed back to the light by a dancing lady in diaphanous garments and returns to the real world, having at last secured her parents' attention.

It is an undeniably sentimental tearjerker, leavened with comic sequences of which the great Maurice Tourneur, brought in to direct, apparently disapproved, but he produced a very beautiful film none the less. With his art director Ben Carré, Tourneur created oversized sets and perspective effects to make the diminutive Mary seem even smaller. The bulk of the credit, though, goes to Pickford herself, whose cinema-specific acting style, honed over the 176 or so films she had already made (and there were many more to come), set a standard, but she was also entirely conversant with every aspect of the business, from lighting to finance, and took control of her productions. Although she did play more mature roles, Pickford recognised that, as for Chaplin's Little Tramp, the 'America's Sweetheart' of the public's affections would take her to the top of her profession. The prospect of $1 million a year and being the most powerful woman in Hollywood were strong inducements.

Dir: Maurice Tourneur; **Scr**: Frances Marion, from the play by Eleanor Gates; **Ph**: John van den Broeck, Lucien Andriot; **Art Dir**: Ben Carré; **Cast**: Mary Pickford, Frank McGlynn Sr, Gladys Fairbanks, Madlaine Traverse, Charles Wellesley.

Premier prix de violoncelle
France, 1907 – 3 mins
Pathé Frères

Film comedy in the earliest days derived from various types of stage comedy and from printed comics. Widely acknowledged as the first was the Lumières' *L'Arroseur arrosée* (translated as 'The Sprinkler Sprinkled' or sometimes 'The Biter Bit'), which was included in the programme of films at the celebrated first commercial projection at the Grand Café in the Place de l'Opéra in Paris on the 28 December 1895. In a simple, classic gag, a young boy treads on a hosepipe, blocking the flow of water; puzzled the gardener looks down the spout, at which point the boy removes his foot, releasing the water and soaking the gardener. This was based on a famous one-page cartoon by Herman Vogel structured in eight pictures (the individual framing of the 'strip' hadn't come into vogue yet), very like a storyboard for many of the comedies that would succeed this early effort by the Lumière brothers. In Vogel's version, which was more complex than the short film, the boy is seen committing this outrage and a crowd of people report it to a passing gendarme, a chase ensues and the boy gets his comeuppance. As films became longer, the chase comedy, which originated from this and also from stage chase scenes in pantomimes, became a major film genre that survived until the more developed style of the character comedians like Max Linder in France and Chaplin in Hollywood began to take over just before World War I.

In the interim, these anarchic knockabout chases were a principal pleasure in the mixed film programme. Generally taking place in the street, the chase was instigated by an accident or misdemeanour leading to ever increasing numbers of people pursuing the instigator – like the story of the goose that laid the golden egg, they are carried along by the chase. There were endless variations on the theme, of which *Premier prix de violoncelle*, made by Pathé, is one example. In this case, the chase becomes vertical as the inhabitants of a multistorey house run up the stairs to throw furniture at a wandering musician who has settled down outside the house to play quite appallingly. The discordant music inspires a corresponding harmony of effort by the residents to shut the creature up and as he continues they throw ever more extreme objects at him from the upper-floor windows. First vases and cushions, followed by whole mattresses and wardrobes – but nothing can stop him, not even a grenade or hosepipe. Eventually, someone has a bright idea – a small girl is sent in to give the musician a bunch of flowers and, with a curtsey, thank him for his marvellous performance. The musician's vanity satisfied, he bows to the company and leaves.

Apart from the clever ending – easy to miss if you are not watching carefully – the pleasures of the film are all in the frenetic pace and energy and the co-operative spirit of the citizens, which are supplied by the stock company of experienced comedians employed by the studio. While the use of stage scenery to represent the street perhaps betrays the theatrical origins of this piece, and though the players remain anonymous, these comedies shouldn't be thought of as unsophisticated.

Prod: Pathé Frères.

The Queen of Spades (*Pikovaya dama*)
Russia, 1916 – 63 mins
Yakov Protazanov

In adapting literary works to the screen, sometimes specific choices have to be made. In the case of adapting the classic Russian story 'The Queen of Spades' by Alexander Pushkin (written in 1834), it was necessary for Russian director Yakov Protazanov to choose how to portray a key incident left vague in the written story – namely, the point when the hero, Herman (or German), sees the dead Countess whom he has terrified into her grave some time before. Is this a supernatural event or is he delusional? In visual terms, this might be portrayed by superimposition, a method well understood in conventional film grammar, suggesting that the figure is either ghostly or a figment of the protagonist's imagination, and indeed this is what the screenwriter chooses to do. The fact that the old Countess walks almost entirely out of the screen before the dissolves takes place (and it is difficult to catch in the most commonly available print) has led some critics to deduce that Protazanov was trying to retain the ambiguity of the written story, whereas he was clearly very conscious of cinematic specificity.

A similar choice was made by Eliot Stannard in a British film called *Lady Audley's Secret* (1920). In the book on which the film was based, we don't learn of the heroine's underlying mercenary motivation, which, as with the character of Herman, will eventually lead to death and madness, until the very end. This would have been impossible to do visually without some very clunky reveal in the final reel, so Stannard chooses to disclose the secret to the audience at the outset, in a title showing her disgust at a shabby hat, but not to the other characters in the story. It's a brave choice but one that can be made to work.

Protazanov also makes another important choice about the adaptation, which is to emphasise the psychological aspects of 'The Queen of Spades', a story about Herman's obsessive search for certainty through the medium of the card game, in which the main character

enters into a kind of Faustian pact to win the riches that will match his
ambition. He is seeking that most elusive of phenomena, the sure thing.
It is implied, though, that he himself, in a proto-Freudian way, is affecting
the turn of events and literally the turn of the cards. The director
consequently places the burden of the storytelling on the actors and the
mise en scène. Unlike the growing trend for dynamic action, most
notable in the style of American film-making, Protazanov chooses to
enhance the depth inherent in the story through the acting, principally as
played by Ivan Mozzhukhin (see variant spelling Mosjoukine), and by the
opulence of the sets, for which he sought the advice of the doyen of
Russian stage design, Alexander Benois, who lent him three assistants,
Vladimir Ballyuzek, Serge Lilienberg and Valere Pshibitnevsky. The choice
of Mozzhukhin was perhaps obvious, as he was the most talented
cinema actor of his age, but in a nice twist of fate, he also conformed
precisely to Pushkin's description of Herman as having 'the profile of a
Napoleon and the soul of a Mephistopheles'. Protazanov certainly makes
the most of the legendary 'Mozzhukhin gaze' in long takes, conveying
the tortured soul of the character. This intelligent adaptation shows us
the sophistication of Russian film-making before the Soviet era – it
deserves to be better known.

Dir: Yakov Protazanov; **Scr**: Yakov Protazanov, Fyodor Otsep, based on the story by
Alexander Pushkin; **Ph**: Yevgeni Slavinsky; **Cast**: Ivan Mozzhukhin, Vera Orlova, Tamara
Duvan, Yelizaveta Shebueva, Nikolai Panov, Pavel Pavlov.

Regen (*Rain*)
Netherlands, 1929 – 12 mins
Joris Ivens, M. H. K. Franken

Joris Ivens's *Regen*, a short study of the effects of a shower of rain on Amsterdam, was immediately dubbed a 'ciné poème' by French critics. Like *Manhatta**, it was unselfconsciously artistic, concerned with the art of describing a truth or making an observation rather than storytelling or polemic. The poetic analogy is a good one, as Ivens himself claims to have been partly inspired by the famous Verlaine poem 'Il Pleure dans mon coeur, comme il pleut sur la ville'. Ivens uses many of the same approaches that a poet would – in the film, he examines minutely the details of the rain in all its facets, paying attention to texture, layers, the focus of the gaze, the point of view, the relationships of light and dark and pattern. He examines the drops of rain in water and on the streets, its effects on the people as they rush for shelter, the even sheen of moisture reflecting off a car bonnet or the gushing of water from a drain. Rhythm is supplied through the editing of the images, and the overall piece has a temporal cohesion based on the shower of rain, from the first few drops, through its furious downpour to the light breaking through the clouds. Ivens also suggests that the way he structured the film had a relationship with the composition of music, and this may be supported by Hanns Eisler's 1941 composition to accompany the film and which responds to different sections of the film as separate musical interludes – the famous bird's-eye shot of a mass of umbrellas is figured as the intermezzo within his *Fourteen Ways of Describing Rain*.

If the method is poetic and the structure musical, then the overall aesthetic is photographic, although arguably this is filtered through the Dutch painterly tradition. Ivens was a photographer turned cinematographer. His father owned a photographic business, and the young Ivens was highly trained in all aspects of the trade, visiting the great factories and laboratories in Germany. It was here that he met Professor Emanuel Goldberg, the developer of the 'Kinamo' (from the

Greek, 'love for cinema'), a compact 35mm spring-driven camera designed to be hand-held. The spring motor meant you didn't need the stability of a tripod to counteract the motion of the cranking. It also meant that Ivens could roam about the streets catching images 'unawares', as Vertov had aspired to with his 'Kino-Pravda' series. The point of view matching precisely to the eye of the cameraman enhanced that sense of the personal vision that Ivens strived for. As with many superficially simple works of art, *Regen* is actually quite complex – it was shot over many, many months and edited with great deliberation. As Ivens recalls in his memoirs:

> At that time, I lived with and for the rain … it was part game, part obsession, part action. I had decided upon several sections of the city I wanted to film and I organised a system of rain watchers, friends who would telephone me from certain sections of town when the rain effects I wanted happened. I never moved without my camera – it was with me in the office, laboratory, street, train. I lived with it and when I slept it was on my bedside table so that if it was raining when I woke up I could film through the studio window over my bed.[27]

Dir: Joris Ivens, M. H. K. Franken; **Ph**: Joris Ivens.

Revolutionshochzeit (The Last Night)
Germany, 1928 – 99 mins
A. W. Sandberg

The representation of time in film is an interesting thing. In this quite
conventional drama, most of the action takes place in the course of one
day and one night, a device that builds tension. In classic Hollywood
cinema, the slowing down of time in the final reel to something nearer
to how it is experienced by humans (real time) is a device used frequently
in action movies to create that edge-of-the-seat feeling.
Revolutionshochzeit (which translates loosely as 'Wedding of the
Revolution'), directed by one of Denmark's finest, Anders Wilhelm
Sandberg, uses 'real time' in its final reels, much of the action confined
to two rooms in a chateau in France in 1797 during the Terror.

An aristocrat, Alaine, has fled from the city with her servant Leontine
(played by the delightful Karina Bell) to her chateau at Tronville, where
she hopes to meet her betrothed, Ernest, a cavalier fighting the French
revolutionaries. To do this, she has swapped identities with Leontine to
obtain passports from the handsome young officer Marc Aron, who
overrides his colleague Montaloup, an agent of the Committee for Public
Safety. She marries Ernest just as the Revolutionary army arrives at the
chateau. Ernest is sentenced immediately by Montaloup to death by
firing squad for fighting his own countrymen, but again Marc Aron
intervenes to let the newly weds have their wedding night.
Ernest unmanfully decides to flee before the clock strikes six in the
morning, the time allotted for his execution. Marc Aron is sent for one
more time and, after showing his contempt for Ernest, agrees to save
him for the sake of Alaine, for whom he feels compassion.
Ernest escapes and Marc Aron takes his place in Alaine's rooms, but
when discovered by Montaloup, he is forced to accept that he has
betrayed the Revolution and must face the firing squad in Ernest's place.

Montaloup, distressed but determined, gives Marc Aron the
remaining hours of the night till the clock strikes six. The passage of time

is represented literally by an elaborate clock on the mantelpiece. Marc Aron is enchanted by the two little Sèvres figurines, a man and a woman, who dance as the hours chime. When Ernest was faced with the prospect of waiting several hours for death, he found it unbearable; Alaine had tried to comfort him by saying that hours can be as years if spent well. Marc Aron is more philosophical, and prepares to spend his last night reading a book of poetry he has found and remains respectfully outside his lady's bedchamber. This gallantry impassions Alaine and a wedding of sorts is consummated – the last thing we see is his hand stopping the ornamental clock, to save his lover from being conscious of the hours ticking away or perhaps to steal time itself. An appealing concept that true love will conquer time, in this case sex outside wedlock with a relative stranger adds a slight frisson. This device of stopping time for such a purpose has been used successfully in later films such as *A Matter of Life and Death* (1946) and *Out of Sight* (1998).

Dir: A. W. Sandberg; **Scr**: Norbert Falk and Robert Liebmann, based on the play *Revolutionsbryllup* by Sophus Michaelis; **Ph**: Christen Jørgensen, Hans Scheib; **Cast**: Gösta Ekman, Diormira Jacobini, Karina Bell, Fritz Kortner, Walter Rilla.

Safety Last!
US, 1923 – 73 mins
Fred Newmeyer, Sam Taylor

Possibly the most famous image of a silent film comedy is of a man in horn-rimmed glasses and a straw boater hanging from the hands of a clock twelve storeys above the street. If you've never heard of Harold Lloyd or *Safety Last!*, you have almost certainly seen this image – it's as famous as Marilyn standing over the subway grill. There is more to *Safety Last!*, however, than this shot. The 'glasses' character developed with great deliberateness by Lloyd is a very clever invention – a modern everyman, neither too clever nor too dumb, good-hearted, aspirational and well intentioned, we identify with him.

There are great moments, such as the sight gag at the very beginning where we see our hero (an intertitle tells us this is the last dawn he will see in Great Bend) behind bars, as if in prison, a noose dangling in the background. As the camera rises out, we see that he is in fact standing at the barrier in a railway station and the noose is the mail catcher for the train. But it is the famous ascent up the building that is most memorable and produces that iconic image. The Boy (Harold) has been lying to his girlfriend about how well he's getting on in the city, but he needs money, so comes up with the idea for a publicity stunt to draw crowds to the department store where he works in return for a reward. He has persuaded his friend, a human fly, to climb the huge building – he will do the first storey, then the friend will take over once people won't be able to tell them apart.

For years, people have debated how this sequence was done – did Harold Lloyd do all the stunts himself; was he really twelve storeys up on that ledge? If the film had been made yesterday rather than (nearly) ninety years ago, we wouldn't even be asking, but it is part of the mythology of early Hollywood that everything was done in a splendidly unconstrained fashion, with stars performing all their own stunts – hanging off skyscrapers, dancing on aeroplane wings or tied to the

railway tracks with an express train coming into view on the horizon. These days, stars can't (apparently) do their own stunts for insurance reasons, which means our suspension of disbelief is somewhat lessened and they have to work harder to convince us their stunt is real and take us into that moment.

Of course, this whole myth about the danger to the star was a carefully constructed marketing ploy. The silent stars may have been less well insured but they weren't stupid. But even if Harold Lloyd didn't really scale that building, it feels like he did. During the climb, as he mounts one storey after another, praying all the time that his friend will rescue him at the next, we are with him every minute. Every stumble makes you gasp. In one horrible moment, his mate, who is being chased up the building by a policeman, manages to throw him a rope, which he catches; thinking he is secure at last, we cut back to see that the end of the rope is not attached to anything. The clock sequence, in which the feeble metal of the second hand bends as he struggles to get his foot on the ledge, the face peeling away, leaking springs, is a triumph. And all the time, the street far, far below remains in sight. Vertigo and film are a great combination.

Dir: Fred Newmeyer, Sam Taylor; **Scr**: Sam Taylor, Hal Roach; **Ph**: Walter Lundin; **Cast**: Harold Lloyd, Mildred Davies, Bill Strother, Noah Young.

(*Opposite page*) Pre insurance: death-defying stunts were a memorable feature of the 1920s film

The Scarecrow
US, 1920 – 19 mins
Buster Keaton, Edward F. Cline

There is something very satisfying about the 19-minute comedy, just like
the 90-minute feature or the 7-minute cartoon. It has a noble history too,
being the typical length of a music-hall turn or sketch. It's long enough to
develop a gag or story, or often two or more interrelated stories (it often
subdivides into 7-minute sections), without wearying an audience used to
variety programmes, as audiences for film were at that time. By 1920,
when *The Scarecrow* was made, the 'two-reeler', as it became known in
the trade, had been developed to a high art by the Hollywood fun
factories. And this episode length of between 19 and 24 minutes is still
the standard unit for comedy today – *The Simpsons*, for example.

My choice of this Buster Keaton short comedy is fairly random – I
could easily have picked one of the brilliant two-reelers he made with
Roscoe Arbuckle, to my mind (at the risk of offending Laurel and Hardy
fans) the best comedy duo of all. I have chosen *The Scarecrow* because
it's a personal favourite of mine and because it shows its comedic roots
derived from circus clowning, pantomime and slapstick, which is a
fascinating subject. However, there is nothing nostalgic about the gags,
but, rather, all the skills of the past have been brought to bear on a very
modern comedy.

The first 7 minutes are glorious. Buster and housemate (Joe Roberts)
share a one-room dwelling kitted out with numerous space-saving
devices so that they can change the room from kitchen, dining room to
parlour to bedroom, and so maintain their bourgeois aspirations to the
typical American home. Objects transform – the flip-up bed becomes a
piano, the sofa a bathtub, the gramophone changes into a range cooker,
and so on – in a style that was characteristic of the pantomime tradition,
in which one object came to look like another. This was done not by
photographic trickery but by the use of stage props and mere suggestion
– so that when Buster picks up the gramophone turntable with a lever

handle, it suggests the round iron cover of a cooker. Belonging more to the circus tradition are the virtuoso juggling and choreography of the dinner sequence. All of the condiments are suspended from the ceiling by string and a series of pulleys, again to save space, and as they eat, the two pass each other various items in a beautifully co-ordinated series of throws which become more elaborate and impressive. Clearing up after dinner, they rearrange the room into the parlour – the washing-up, which is nailed to the tabletop, is hosed down and the scraps automatically drop through a chute to the pigpen outside; likewise, the tub empties its water into a miniature duck pond in the yard, and once clean, the tabletop reverses to become a picture motto hanging on the wall.

The rest of the comedy concerns Buster and Joe's rivalry for the hand of the farmer's daughter (Sybil Seely) and is constructed around a long chase involving a cream pie, a (not) mad dog (played by Arbuckle's dog Luke), an enraged farmer (played by Keaton's father), a pretend scarecrow, a misunderstanding over a proposal (Buster was just kneeling to do up a bootlace) and a marriage conducted on a motorbike. Keaton, by this time, had perfected the stone face and is impeccable. The film demonstrates the perfect formula for success – 'comedy, love and a bit with a dog'.

Dir/Scr: Buster Keaton, Edward F. Cline (as Eddie Cline); **Ph**: Elgin Lessley; **Cast**: Buster Keaton, Joe Keaton, Joe Roberts, Sybil Seely, Luke the dog.

Sex in Chains (*Geschlecht in Fesseln*)
Germany, 1928 – 107 mins
Wilhelm Dieterle

There is little direct portrayal of homosexuality in the silent era.
Self-censorship prevented the vast majority of film-makers from taking it
as a subject or even alluding to it. The very few unambiguous references
(i.e. aside from the odd eccentrically dressed nightclub-goer) all seem to
appear in films made in Germany during the relatively liberal Weimar era.
The first, *Different from the Others*, was made, astonishingly, in 1919.
Wilhelm Dieterle's provocatively titled *Sex in Chains* was made nearly a
decade later when film-making techniques had improved, although the
same could not be said for the treatment of same-sex relations. It is
essentially a social-problem film but arguably the theme of prison reform
indicated by the subtitle, 'The sexual plight of prisoners', is a convenient
device for looking at homosexuality, although the issue of prison reform
is given due weight. The opening titles declare the source material to be
Franz Höllering's work on sexual behaviour in prison and Karl Plättner's
first-hand testimony *Eros in Prison*. Either way, it was a bold move from
the young actor turned director Dierterle, who would go on to have a
glittering Hollywood career thanks to his real film-making talent.

Even by late Weimar German standards, this film is beautifully
crafted. In the opening scenes, we discover the desperate financial straits
of the newlyweds via a visit from the young wife Helene's bourgeois
father. She is caught with duster in hand and has to pretend that it is the
maid's day off; her father gives her an engraved silver cake slice – a most
useless object – while she pretends to call her husband's office on the
disconnected phone. When the unemployed Franz returns home, he sees
the cake slice and bites on it – we can't eat it, it says, without the need
for a clunky title. Dieterle, as well as playing the lead with 'method'-like
skill, uses every bit of elegant film grammar in the book. In a beautifully
observed sequence that reflects the couple's mature relationship, he
caves in to his wife's entreaties that she be allowed to get a job,

although he feels unmanned. When called upon to defend her against a man who is harassing her, he hits him and is arrested. But when the man dies, he is imprisoned.

The issue of sexual frustration is raised immediately when he is confined to a cell with three other men and dreams of making love to his wife, rendered in big close-up and soft focus; on waking, he strides in a rage to the door but finds it locked. The understanding old lag tells him it will pass but that he has known men 'unman' themselves just to get some sleep. This is the crux of the film – frustrated sexual desire coupled with the need for affection. One inmate kills himself because of it. It also affects Helene, who finds it equally unbearable, going to the prison one night and pounding on the doors screaming for her man. In desperation she turns to the friend who has helped her to get a job – arriving on his doorstep with one word on her lips, 'Mann' (variously 'husband' or 'man'), but her meaning is clear. The equivalent crisis point occurs in the cell when Alfred, a young new inmate, arrives. He falls for Franz and in the middle of the night declares his passion, and we see their hands clasp each other. After his release, Franz and Helene can barely speak to each other but, far from being judgmental, the film lays the inevitable breakdown of the marriage at the door of a penal system that didn't allow conjugal visits. When Alfred knocks at Franz's door, Helene recognises the situation immediately, suggesting that a general awareness of homosexuality, even among the delicately reared, was not uncommon.

Dir: Wilhelm Dieterle; **Scr**: Hanns Heinz Ewers, Georg C. Klaren, Herbert Juttke; **Ph**: Robert Lach; **Cast**: Wilhelm Dieterle, Mary Johnson, Gunnar Tolnaes, Paul Henckels, Hans Heinrich von Twardowski.

The Smiling Madame Beudet (*La Souriante Madame Beudet*)
France, 1923 – 35 mins
Germaine Dulac

Germaine Dulac was an experienced and skilled film-maker (not to mention critic, theorist, feminist, union activist and supporter of film societies) who was completely immersed in the arts and artistic movements of the period. The specificities of the cinema were of particular interest to her in conveying the frustration of the artistic soul, particularly of women, struggling against the conventions of bourgeois society. Dulac is sometimes seen as difficult to understand, possibly because many of us see her most inaccessible film, *The Seashell and the Clergyman* (1928), first, presented as an example of surrealism in film, but *The Smiling Madame Beudet* is very accessible. If we have to put an '-ism' to it, it should be Impressionism. Another '-ism' that applies is feminism, as it is told entirely from the woman's point of view. Concerning a bourgeois housewife of refined intellectual tastes, who lives in a small town with her conventional and vulgar husband, it expresses, to some extent, dissatisfaction with the status quo. However, it presents neither a solution to the woman's problem in legalistic terms of more relaxed divorce or labour legislation nor any abuse, other than the ennui of marriage and the stifling bourgeois world in which she is trapped – but so trapped that she contemplates the extreme solution of murder.

It sounds rather melodramatic, but in tackling the adaptation of *The Smiling Madame Beudet*, Dulac marshals all the techniques of French Impressionism – superimposition and distortions, unusual angles and cutting, clever set dressing and lighting – to convey the inner turmoil of the frustrated housewife without histrionics. Her desires are represented visually – the sunlight reflecting on water representing the music she craves; the handsome tennis pro pictured in a magazine she is reading, who emerges in her imagination (in a superimposition) live from the page to haul the detested husband bodily from her sight. Her repressed irritation is initially manifested in nothing more dramatic than the moving of a vase of flowers from the centre of the table, where her husband repeatedly replaces it, to her preferred, more artistically pleasing, position at its side. But the husband's recurring 'joke' of putting a gun to his head wears thin, while his thoughtless, or possibly spiteful, act of locking the piano before going out, thus depriving her of her one solace, tips Mme Beudet over the edge. Her sense of claustrophobia becomes personified in the imagined figure of her husband, whose distorted form we see looming towards her in slow motion, grimacing horribly. In a state of

The dreariness of bourgeois marriage incites rebellion

desperation, she loads his gun with bullets, but when the husband repeats the familiar old joke, ironically he turns the gun on her instead.

The play of the same name, on which the film is based, makes greater comic use of this irony, whereas Dulac uses it to make a more sober feminist statement. The play was written according the tenets of the *école du silence*, a practice in which the dialogue does not express the characters' real thoughts or attitudes. Without the facility of spoken dialogue to convey the contrast between the outer expressions and inner thoughts of the character, Dulac uses clever visual techniques to convey that dichotomy in the film, and, in doing so, arguably created the first truly feminist film. Madame Beudet's tragedy is that, as a woman, she is trapped in a world without possible escape where even an attempt to murder her husband only occasions more of his platitudes. Her middle-distance stare expresses complete hopelessness – she is not smiling.

Dir: Germaine Dulac; **Scr**: André Obey, from the play by André Obey and Denys Amiel; **Ph**: Maurice Foster, Paul Parguel; **Cast**: Germaine Dermoz, Alexandre Arquillière, Jean d'Yd, Yvette Grisier, Madeleine Guitty.

The Son of the Sheik
US, 1926 – 67 mins
George Fitzmaurice

There are many reasons to make fun of *The Son of the Sheik*. The plot is implausible, some of the acting is not great and the action sequences are largely derived from Douglas Fairbanks's *The Mark of Zorro* (1921). Apart from some very good set designs (by William Cameron Menzies), the film is quite ordinary, with one major exception, which is Rudolph Valentino.

Star quality is often indefinable, which is part of its attraction, but sheer physical beauty would almost account for all of Valentino's appeal. What raised him to the level of an icon, which still holds power today, was a confluence of factors: charm and an engaging screen personality, the perfection of his screen kiss, the dancer's physique and a tragically early death at thirty-one that inspired an outpouring of hysteria we associate only with Chaplin or the Beatles. The impact of all this physical perfection in a romantic role that so complemented his image must have been heady stuff to the newly emancipated female audience seated in the semi-privacy of the darkened cinema and allowed a really good, long, hard look. No role could be more complementary for the dark, handsome Italian Valentino than *The Sheik* (1921) and its remake, *The Son of the Sheik*. The original film, based on the bestselling novel by English writer Edith M. Hull, contained just enough of the novel's scurrilous content to appeal to the sizeable audience for Hollywood films by the early 1920s.

The story, a blueprint for every romantic novel of its type since, concerns an independent-spirited western heroine, who, on a visit to the Arabian desert, engages in a battle of wills with a handsome sheik and is captured and raped/seduced (implied in the film, explicit in the book). The sequel, written five years later, poses a somewhat similar storyline, with the Sheik (son of the original, and both played by Valentino) falling for a native dancer whom he mistakenly believes has lured him to a rendezvous where he was attacked and tortured by the wandering gang

'Rudolph
Valentin
again
'She

of brigands who force her nightly to dance for wealthy clients. In revenge, he kidnaps her and carries her off to his lavish tent in the desert, tearing open his robes to reveal the whiplashes on his chest. This time the rape is more directly implied, as he pushes her towards the bed, blocking the camera's view. After the cut, we see her, tearful, on the bed – no rescue is suggested. As in the first film, this is made 'alright' by the fact that the couple are in love, with the implication of eventual marriage.

Building on the reaction to the first film, the film-makers use every opportunity to titillate the audience – the torture scene where Valentino is hung up bare-chested, in ripped robes, holds a powerful erotic charge even now. This was the beginning of a Hollywood formula that has plied us with beautiful young men ever since. The banality of the surrounding film has always been irrelevant.

Dir: George Fitzmaurice; **Scr**: Frances Marion, Fred de Gresac; **Ph**: George Barnes; **Art Dir**: William Cameron Menzies; **Cast**: Rudolph Valentino, Vilma Bànky, Agnes Ayres, Carl Dane, Montague Love.

(*Opposite page*) Rape fantasy replay with the greatest matinée idol of them all, Rudolph Valentino

The Spirit of His Forefathers
UK, *c.*1900 – 30 seconds
British Mutoscope and Biograph Company

Innovative, gimmicky and short, advertising was a natural fit with early cinema. Like early films, the first advertisements were part of a bigger collection of multimedia products: in the case of *The Spirit of His Forefathers*, a print and poster campaign based on a commissioned painting of 1894 by Matthew B. Hewerdine. The painting depicts a Scottish laird relaxing with a glass of Dewar's whisky and surrounded by the framed portraits of his ancestors. Called forth, perhaps by the aroma of the whisky, several of the figures are climbing out of their frames to join their descendant in a toast to Queen Victoria. It is a clever illustration, reinforcing the image of Scotland, with its tartan and castles, and the connection with the monarch as the Jubilee celebrations approached. Most of all, it is the intriguing device of the frame-within-the-frame and the breaking free of the inanimate into the world of the living, which is itself a picture in a frame. Lynda Nead's concept of the haunted gallery emphasises the neatness of the similarity between the wall full of pictures and film:

> A space for pictures and for ghosts, the gallery is also for endless pacing watched by portraits of generations of the dead. It is a place of presences but not life, of likenesses … How apt that the shadows cast on the ceiling by the windows and tapestried walls look like a strip of film, with intermittent, spaced-out picture frames, separated by short intervals of blank darkness. Set this sequence in motion and the enchantment begins; the pictures come to life and the ghosts haunt the gallery.[28]

Like breaking the fourth wall in the theatre, breaking out of the frame is a device that has been used sparingly in film over the decades – I well remember the surprise of seeing a character stepping out of the cinema frame in Woody Allen's *The Purple Rose of Cairo* (1985), and more recently, the delightfully underplayed use of moving images in the framed pictures in Hogwarts Castle in the *Harry Potter* films (other examples are *Blade Runner* [1982], *The Cameraman* [1928], *My Own Private Idaho* [1991], etc.). As the living billboard becomes commonplace, the device may lose some of its impact, but back in 1900 it was innovative enough for the advertising campaign to inspire this novelty film from the British Mutoscope and Biograph Company, a British offshoot of the pioneering American company run by W. K. L. Dickson in London.

Like other Biograph films, it was a large-format (roughly 68mm) high-quality production filmed at the open-air studio just off the Strand. It depicted a two-tiered set of picture frames from which the actors, playing the kilted ancestors, spring down. The film adds a temporal dimension; only after the Laird has drunk some whisky does he see the 'ancestors', leaving open to interpretation whether they are real, or a scotch-induced hallucination. It works well as a film outside of its advertising context and is, in fact, a refinement of a previous American film that was a direct promotion for the Dewar's brand back in 1897. Produced by the International Film Company as a publicity stunt and projected onto a gigantic hoarding in Herald Square in New York, it was presumably sanctioned by 'Tommy' Dewar, a pioneering 'ad man' who was busy turning Dewar's into a global brand.

Before the 1920s and the consolidation of the cinema exhibition sector, advertising films were rather ad hoc elements of a wider campaign, but they retained their short running time (30 seconds, then as now) and their ingenuity in playing with the medium's specificity.

Prod Co: British Mutoscope and Biograph Company.

Stachka (*Strike*)
USSR, 1925 – 90 mins
Sergei M. Eisenstein

Eisenstein's first solo feature film is an astonishing debut. Intended as the first of a multi-part epic chronicling the rise of the proletariat, this was the only episode of the more broadly conceived story to make it to the screen but is indicative of the scope of Eisenstein's, not always realised, artistic ambition.

The plot concerns a strike in the factory district of an unnamed city in pre-Revolutionary Russia and a straight conflict between capital and labour. There are no stars or personal trajectories drawn here, characters are, on the whole, representative, or types: the corpulent boss, the cunning police informer, the noble union leader, the vulnerable child. The social classes act in their predetermined ways – the workers combine and set up ever more ingenious secret meetings, the foremen blab and bully, the informants lie and creep about, the bosses put out press releases, paying lip service to negotiation and hiring criminal agents provocateurs to discredit the workers before finally calling in the military to stamp them out for good.

In film-making terms, this is not the formal poetry or 'Kino Eye' of Vertov but what Eisenstein later called the 'kino fist'. From the first moments of the film, the audience is thrust into this relentless movement, with the persistent motion of the machines and human beings scurrying about. The camera angles chop and change, with the full range of tilts and upward shots, close-ups and teeming crowd scenes. The editing pace is frenetic, but as well as the movement and action, which was at least in part dictated by the performance style (known as 'eccentric' acting), Eisenstein also uses montage in the Kuleshov sense, in one example juxtaposing the police informants, with their exotic pseudonyms of 'the fox' or 'the owl', by the use of dissolves to an image of those actual animals. Amid the wild cutting, this has a curiously old-fashioned feel. Similarly, the now notorious juxtaposition of images of the workers being cut down by mounted cavalry with a cow being slaughtered in unrelentingly gory detail feels over-deliberate to us now, whereas the almost comic scene of the king of the thieves (like some modern-day version of Ali Baba calling his gang out of the hundreds of wine barrels in which they are hiding) could have come straight out of a Fellini movie. The final scenes, in which the mounted soldiers, like stormtroopers silhouetted against the sky, invade the workers' tenement buildings cutting them off from escape, are truly chilling. The concluding message conveyed in the title, 'Don't Forget', is as powerful as it could be.

Dir: Sergei M. Eisenstein; **Scr**: Sergei M. Eisenstein, Grigori Aleksandrov; **Ph**: Eduard Tissé; **Cast**: members of the Proletkult Theatre.

Stage Struck
US, 1925 – 78 mins
Allan Dwan

The opening scene of *Stage Struck*, a vehicle for the great silent screen star Gloria Swanson, is an exotic colour spectacle in two-strip Technicolor. The first title before the appearance of the actress in a sumptuous velvet gown with a huge jewelled headdress says simply, 'The greatest actress of all time'. For those who know Gloria Swanson from her defining role as Norma Desmond in the 1950 film *Sunset Blvd.*, her connection with the glory days of the silent screen ('We didn't need dialogue. We had faces') might seem fitting, until we realise that this opening sequence, in which she acts the part of a glamour queen, is pastiche. Here, Swanson is ridiculing her real-life penchant for fine clothes and ambitions to be a serious actress. Portraying herself as Salome and holding aloft the head of John the Baptist on a platter, in a match-shot dissolve she becomes 'Jenny Hagen whose dreams were all of triumphs as an actress and whose life was all long hours for poor pay in a cheap restaurant' holding a tray with a plate of beans.

The object of Jenny's affections is the handsome short-order cook, Orme, played by Lawrence Gray. He is obsessed with actresses and seems to barely notice Jenny and so she is learning to be an emotional actress by correspondence course. This manual of bad acting gives instructions to be practised at home where, over the ironing, she must 'Register the look of a contented wife' and 'Throw yourself at the door. You cry "abandoned!, abandoned!" Then faint.' Of course, she's terrible, and it's a nice twist – the Swanson of Norma Desmond portrayed as a talentless skivvy, desperate to impress the boy next door with her artistry but getting only laughs. Desmond's celebrated line from the final shot of *Sunshine Blvd.*, 'I'm ready for my close-up, Mr DeMille', reinforces our

(*Opposite page*) Gloria Swanson, untypically unglamorous, dreams of being … like Gloria Swanson

association of her with great classical roles, but although she made several films with the legendary director, they were mostly marital comedies like *Male and Female* (1919), during which she famously had to act in a cage with a live lion. I've seen this clip described as 'typical of DeMille's brash and extravagant biblical epics'. Except it isn't. It's another fantasy sequence in a comedy – a version of J. M. Barrie's *The Admirable Crichton*.

Stage Struck, then, is Gloria Swanson doing what she does best as an accomplished comic actress at the height of her career, expressing through the character her desire to be a dramatic actress. It's a good comedy and she is delightful in it; during the restaurant scenes, she even does some slapstick, a form she claimed to despise. As a youngster in 1916, she once had a bit part in a Chaplin comedy (*His New Job*) but didn't stay on, as she had no desire to become a comedienne. In the end, she spent most of her career playing in romantic comedy features, and if she did eventually get to play a few serious roles, it was because she took charge of her own career and produced them herself through United Artists – *Sadie Thompson* (1928) was the most successful. So, that pastiche opening sequence in *Stage Struck* looks forward to a Gloria Swanson who will never exist, and twenty-five years later, she plays a Gloria Swanson who never was, but to such great effect that we are completely convinced – which has to be the sign of a great actress.

Dir: Allan Dwan; **Ph**: George Webber; **Scr**: Forrest Halsey; **Cast**: Gloria Swanson, Lawrence Gray, Ford Sterling, Gertrude Astor.

The Student of Prague (*Der Student von Prag*)
Germany, 1913 – 84 mins
Stellan Rye

Unheimlich is a good word. It's the perfect word to describe the genuinely creepy *The Student of Prague*. Literally, *heimlich* means secret or hidden, so that *unhemlich* implies something that should remain hidden, something unnatural, uncanny. It also carries the meaning of something familiar yet alien at the same time – a concept that would become a horror staple (think of 'Uncle Ira isn't Uncle Ira', from *Invasion of the Bodysnatchers* [1956]). In the case of *The Student of Prague*, the cause of fear and anxiety is not an alien from another planet but the alien within, the *Doppelgänger*.

Balduin, the student protagonist, is the finest swordsman in Prague but lacks money. He is in love with a Countess far above his station and so, when he is approached by Scapinelli, he is tempted into a pact with this Faustian devil, signing away the contents of his student's room for the sum of 100,000 gold coins. The key moment comes when Scapinelli demands his reflection from the mirror in exchange. In a simple but stunningly effective trick shot, the student's reflection walks out of the mirror and follows Scapinelli out. The sense of *unheimlich* is conveyed by Paul Wegener's vacant expression and the stiff walk that he would develop for *The Golem**. From then on, the student is confronted by his double at all key moments, preventing him from wooing the Countess or enjoying his new-found wealth. Society shuns him, sensing this air of unnaturalness. Worse, the double will do 'the deed he swore not to do', arriving early and killing an opponent in a duel, breaking a promise the student made to the family of his adversary. Later, the double appears in the Countess's room, when she sees in her mirror that Balduin has no reflection.

The intertitles, meanwhile, maintain a Poe-like style of narration taken from Alfred de Musset's poem 'The December Night', with its constant refrain, 'a front I spied on ev'ry track,/a stranger there in clothing black,/ like me – It might my brother be'. The poem emphasises the precise physical resemblance, as does Poe's story 'William Wilson' on which the writer Hanns Heinz Ewers, at least partially, based the script. Sources and influences abound for the *Doppelgänger* theme – Ewers's own work (*Alraune* has related themes), Faust clearly, Oscar Wilde's *The Picture of Dorian Gray*, the work of E. T. A. Hoffmann and Dostoevsky, to name a few; and influenced *by* this film was Freud's 'The Uncanny', published in 1919, the stories of H. P. Lovecraft and every vampire film in which the creature has no mirror image. The Guignol design, based on sketches by Klaus Richter, and its location in that most medieval of *Mitteleuropa* cities, Prague, sets the aesthetic tone for most later horror films, but it is not an Expressionist film in the strictest sense. Stellan Rye, the Danish director imported by Ewers for the job, and cameraman Guido Seeber do make extensive use of sombre lighting in both interior and exterior settings, but like *Nosferatu**, there is no resort to the distorted perspective of sets – the design is exemplary, simple and effective, and real. The device of having two images of the same actor in the same frame at the same time is the key to its success, and it is that sense of reality that makes the film all the more unsettling.

Dir: Stellan Rye; **Scr**: Hanns Heinz Ewers; **Ph**: Guido Seeber, from sketches by Klaus Richter; **Cast**: Paul Wegener, John Gottowt, Greta Berger, Lyda Salmonova.

Sunrise: A Song of Two Humans
US, 1927 – 106 mins
F. W. Murnau

It has been noted elsewhere in this volume that silent cinema as a hybrid
art form shares some ground with melodrama and opera. This is
particularly apparent with the works of F. W. Murnau and is useful in
thinking about *Sunrise*, which many consider his finest film. The clue is in
the title 'Sunrise', indicating that this is an uplifting tale, and its subtitle,
'A Song of Two Humans', suggesting an appeal to the emotions that one
might expect of a melodrama or opera. The open credits are equally
revealing – the characters are labelled 'man' (George O'Brien), 'wife'
(Janet Gaynor) and 'woman from the city' (Margaret Livingston) – so that
we know we are in the world of fable and far from realism. Indeed, the
plot is slightly ludicrous. It is established in the opening scene that we are
in 'Summertime, vacation time', with its inference of temporary
pleasures, but one encounter has gone on an unnaturally long time – the
predatory 'woman from the city' lingers in the country to drive the 'man',
mad with lust-driven passion, to murder his wife. Her motives are not
explained – she is presented as cat-like (in one scene, she is even shown
crouched in a tree spying on the world), and is amusing herself with the
expectation of easy-got luxury.

But this is not her story; it is about the gradual reawakening of love
between man and wife. That operatic quality is called to mind in a little
flashback scene, evoked by a chorus of neighbours, of the couple as
newlyweds, happy as children playing with their baby. This is
counterpoised with the present, as the man broods in the kitchen, his
thoughts on the other woman, who is superimposed, draped erotically
over him clutching at his heart. It is as if the camera, in visualising the
weight of burden he feels, is standing in for the aria delivered with an
emotional intensity that we would more commonly attribute to the tale
of a Nordic prince or classical hero. The pivotal point comes with the
dreadful moment of high drama when he contemplates drowning his

submissive and doll-like wife in the lake. When she flees from him, he pursues her to the big city and begs forgiveness; he rediscovers her amid the distractions and delights of the city that had formerly been part of the attraction of the other woman, the imagery here again supplying the unspoken words of the 'song' as the two fall in love once more. As they return home across the lake, the couple are faced with the real threat of a storm, during which, with horrible irony, it appears that the wife has drowned.

The story is simple but heartfelt and moral. As with most truly great films, every part of the production acts in concert like the sections of a well-rehearsed orchestra. The script, adapted from Hermann Suderman's novel *A Trip to Tilsit*, meshes with the design, particularly of the titles, which are sparsely used (but brilliant), and the cityscapes and rural lakeside, which don't entirely look like modern America, adding to that feeling of a stage setting. The acting is very fine (Janet Gaynor won an Academy Award for her performance), but the camerawork is the real star – not flashy but elegant and expensive. Charles Rosher and Karl Struss were also recognised for the film's 'look', the first incidentally issued on the new panchromatic stock. Struss experimented with a beautiful travelling camera shot filmed on an aerial runway allowing the viewer to glide effortlessly through the action. Murnau, with his experience of the best that the German studio system could offer, had been given complete creative control by William Fox and he used it to the full to create this epitome of the silent film art just as the shift to sound film began.

Dir: F. W. Murnau; **Scr**: Carl Mayer; **Ph**: Charles Rosher, Karl Struss; **Art Dir**: Rochus Gliese; **Cast**: George O'Brien, Janet Gaynor, Margaret Livingston.

Suspense
US, 1913 – 12 mins
Lois Weber, Phillips Smalley

The title of this film, *Suspense*, its themes and construction inevitably invite
comparisons with the 'master of suspense', Alfred Hitchcock, and his
fascination with the techniques of audience manipulation. The comparison
is a useful one – Hitchcock, still popular with succeeding generations, can
act as a bridge between what may seem a hopelessly obscure short film
from the silent days and popular film-making today. The techniques used
to create tension in Bond or *Bourne* films are identical to those used in
many Hitchcock films and in Lois Weber and Phillips Smalley's 12-minute
film of 1913. Broadly speaking, this involves devices such as cross-cutting
between simultaneous action, allowing the audience a privileged view,
an increase of pace through editing rhythm, novel perspectives and well
thought through narrative logic. *Suspense* displays all of these features in a
highly condensed film in which no frame is wasted – indeed, in one
celebrated scene, exposition is further condensed even *within* the frame as
it is split three ways to show three concurrent actions (this had been done
previously – see *White Slave Trade**).

The plot is a familiar one that had been used several times in
previous films. A young mother and child living in a remote location are
threatened by a tramp in the absence of the hard-working man of the
house. Frightened by the discovery of the tramp prowling around the
house (we get a privileged view of him first, heightening the tension),
the wife rings her husband (this is where the split screen comes in) as the
tramp enters the kitchen and proceeds to first satisfy his hunger and
then, clutching the knife from the kitchen table, breaks into the rest of
the house. Meanwhile, the husband, racing from the office, jumps into a
nearby car and drives hell-for-leather to rescue his wife and child.
The man whose car he has stolen pursues him, along with a number of
convenient policemen, and from here on, the scenes of the chase and
the tramp breaking through her barricaded doors are intercut with

Condensed action in Lois Weber and Phillips Smalley's beautifully crafted thriller

increasing pace. One of the novel perspectives is a close-up of the tramp's arm groping for the lock through a hole punched in the door, a 'Here's Johnny!' moment now familiar from a thousand horror films.

Every attempt is made to condense actions, so that (in another novel perspective) the husband's speeding car is shown in the same frame with the pursuit vehicle reflected in the wing mirror; not only that, but the pursuit vehicle then sharply recedes into the distance as the husband's car speeds up – very clever. The final scene is masterly in its efficiency: the pursuing police fire warning shots at the car thief husband, which are 'heard' by the tramp just as he reaches the now hysterical wife; his attempts to flee are thwarted by the husband charging up the stairs, who, after a brief fight, hands the tramp over to the police and consoles his weeping wife, while simultaneously justifying the theft of his car to the owner.

Knowing what will happen doesn't lessen the tension for the audience, and it was this ability to combine genuine edge-of-the-seat suspense with the required crassness of the happy ending that made Hitchcock bankable with the film studios, and it also worked for Lois Weber in her day. She, like Hitchcock, insisted on total editorial control and resented studio influence, asking in an interview of 1916, 'What other artist has his work interfered with by someone else?'

Dir: Lois Weber, Phillips Smalley; **Cast**: Lois Weber, Valentine Paul, Sam Kaufman, Douglas Gerard.

The Talisman (*Pied de mouton*)
France, 1907 – 15 mins
Albert Capellani

In the early part of the twentieth century, the entertainment you would
probably most aspire to see would be one of the great spectacular
theatrical fantasies of the day. If you couldn't afford it, you might get a
glimpse of its splendours in a féerie, or fairy film, at the cinematograph
shows in the towns or the fairground. This early genre was produced
throughout the 1900s, principally by the Pathé Frères company, to
capitalise on the popularity of the stage shows, cement the company's
cultural aspirations and exploit the attributes of the new medium.
And even though the short film was only a bite-sized piece, it seems to
have caught on rapidly – not unlike the current YouTube phenomenon.
Today, these films are all the more fragmentary, rarely surviving in their
complete form.

What stuns modern-day audiences about these films, which are
quite specific to that period of film history (they were gone by 1912), is
first the colour, for the jewel-like, saturated colours of Pathé's stencilling
process are striking. Second, they tend not to make much sense
narratively speaking, being either a series of tableaux or a kind of
episodic journey. Many féeries are based on familiar fairy tales such as
Cinderella, Aladdin or the Goose That Laid the Golden Eggs, so that the
audience has some idea of settings and the story. With others, the story
is less familiar but of that same genre of fantasy storytelling. The films
incorporate elements of staging derived from the theatrical productions
which may baffle audiences today – ballets were particularly popular,
also grand apotheoses featuring happy-ever-after weddings or parades.
Tricks and transformations of all sorts, which would have been
impressive on stage and relied on elaborate stage machinery, traps of all
kinds, moving scenery, water and fire effects, translated well to film.
Colour and photographic trickery could also be introduced to heighten
the spectacle.

Pied de mouton is a fairly typical example of the genre, although there were many variations. Directed by Albert Capellani and photographed by the talented Segundo de Chomón, it tells the tale of Leonora, who is being forced by her father to marry an ugly old man rather than Gusman, the young hero she loves. The good primrose fairy finds Gusman in despair and gives him a magical sheep's foot, which he uses, during his adventures to recover Leonora, to effect many transformations. In one of these, he rides on a giant yellow snail, which then transforms into a double-bass case; this kind of trick derives from the English pantomime and harlequinade tradition in which objects with some formal similarity – the shape of a snail's shell and a double-bass case – are transformed from one to the other. It is easy to see why the Surrealists were so entranced by these films. Out of the case comes a quartet of ladies with guitars to serenade Leonora, who is on a balcony. At a wave of the magic talisman, the balcony sinks to the ground (on a kind of collapsible set) and then raises Gusman up to his sweetheart's window.

Further adventures ensue as the lovers are chased by the palace guards until they reach the 'grotto of poppies' where, during their drug-induced slumbers, the guards catch up with them. The ugly old man steals the talisman and kidnaps Leonora, but another timely intervention by the primrose fairy saves the lovers, and the hero's retaliation (involving, bizarrely, a troupe of acrobatic kitchen gnomes) persuades the father to consent to their marriage. The final apotheosis sees the couple surrounded by the corps de ballet dressed as Watteau shepherdesses.

Dir: Albert Capellani; **Ph and Tricks**: Segundo de Chomón.

The Thief of Bagdad
US, 1924 – 140 mins
Raoul Walsh

Fantasy film is notoriously difficult to define but instantly recognisable, and Douglas Fairbanks's *The Thief of Bagdad* is definitely one. Drawn freely from the stories of the *Arabian Nights*, the film is noted for two things: the exuberance of Fairbanks as an actor and the glorious art deco design by William Cameron Menzies.

Like his previous swashbuckler, *Robin Hood* (1922), the choice of such a popular subject was one that suited not only Fairbanks's physical style of performance but also his film-making ambitions – big, expensive and hopefully lucrative. It was very much Fairbanks's own project, despite the starry names in the credits such as Cameron Menzies and Raoul Walsh – he developed the script and production design as well as the special effects with which the film was loaded. It took to their logical conclusion the flights of fantasy of the great spectacles of the nineteenth-century theatre, opera and ballet, absorbing also the visual representations of the *Thousand and One Nights* from book illustrations such as those of Edmund Dulac, as well as two centuries of Orientalism in western design, costume and décor. The vast sets were the largest yet built for a film and were reputedly influenced by two German films, *Der müde Tod* (1921) and *Wachsfigurenkabinett*, although the latter was released in the same year. There is no pretence at realism: the scale of buildings are exaggerated sometimes five times as high as the human figures, the perfectly flat floors are highly polished and there are layers upon layers of intricate tracery in the veils of the princess or the light reflected through pierced lanterns and screens. The extravagance continues, with thousands of extras used in the final scenes.

It's all very impressive but would be less effectual without the boundless energy of Fairbanks as the thief leaping around the set with balletic, masculine grace, gesturing grandly and laughing uproariously. He is a joy to watch. The story is good, too, with the happy-go-lucky thief struck down by love for the Caliph's daughter and obliged to go through a series of trials (there is a touch of *L'Inferno** about it) to find a rare treasure and win the hand of the princess. He must overcome his poor status and the competition of rival princes, including the splendid Sôjin, who plays the evil king of the Mongols who is out to capture Bagdad, aided by the gorgeous Anna May Wong as the princess's treacherous handmaiden. After a whirlwind of fantastical episodes with magic carpets and flying horses, enchanted forests and captivating mermaids, the thief, now Prince Ahmed, has a final piece of magic to perform: throwing dust from a magic chest, he calls forth an army of tens of thousands in white livery, pennants flying, to rescue the city and win the princess's hand.

The big production values of *The Thief of Bagdad* set the tone for all fantasy films to come, and even though the effects have been outdone in realism and scope, the childlike imaginativeness is as enchanting now as it was then.

Dir: Raoul Walsh; **Scr**: James T. O'Donohoe, from a story by Douglas Fairbanks (as Elton Thomas); **Art Dir**: William Cameron Menzies; **Cast**: Douglas Fairbanks, Julanne Johnston, Sôjin, Snitz Edwards, Anna May Wong.

The Three-Must-Get-Theres
US, 1922 – 40 mins
Max Linder

Long before Charlie Chaplin, Buster Keaton and Fatty Arbuckle, there
was a whole generation of early film comedians who featured regularly
in their own series under comic pseudonyms – André Deed as 'Boireau'
in France and 'Cretinetti' in Italy, Fred Evans as 'Pimple' in Britain,
Ferdinand Guillaume as Tontolini or Polidor in Italy. Of these, only one
made international status, Max Linder. In fact, it was André Deed's
departure from Pathé in 1909 that allowed Linder to step into his shoes.
Moreover, Linder was the only one of these earlier comedians still in
business as a performer by the time his parody *The Three-Must-Get-
Theres* was made. Untypical of his prewar films, in which his 'Max'
character is a debonair man about town, in top hat and spats, it is a
parody of the famous historical romance by Alexandre Dumas and of the
recently released Fairbanks film *The Three Musketeers* (1921). Nearly all
of the early comedians did parodies and many great silent films were
spoofed – particularly the epics and adventure films, as they provided
situations ripe for comic invention. *The Three-Must-Get-Theres* was the
Airplane (1980) of its day, comprising a rapid succession of linguistic
puns and visual gags. Linder, of course, plays Dart-in-Again, a wannabee
musketeer up from the country in search of adventure.

The opening scene features some excellent stunts from Jazbo the
horse, who tips his master out of the saddle and sits on his hunkers,
refusing to be parted from the farm's black-and-white cow. The horse
makes Dart-in-Again an object of ridicule, but he soon rallies with the
prospect of fighting the dastardly Cardinal Richie-Lou (Duke of
Stichelieu), played with great menace by Bull Montana, a pro wrestler
turned actor. Other great scenes include anachronisms like Constance,
the lady-in-waiting, enlivening the dotty Queen of France's evenings by
playing the ukulele, as well as the plethora of telephones and cars dotted
around the palace and countryside as the Musketeers (Porpoise, Walrus

and Octopus) battle the Cardinal's men. Linder is impressively athletic, pulling off a number of acrobatic moves and pratfalls worthy of Fairbanks himself. He is also personable, with a killer smile, and a good swordsman – some of his best moves occur in the fight scenes. In an especially good sequence, Dart-in-Again is surrounded by a ring of swordsmen, their foils at his throat. When they pull back to impale him, he ducks and they all stab each other, falling dead in a perfect circle.

Linder was a phenomenally precise physical comedian able to produce good three-reel comedies in Hollywood. He was courted by Chaplin, who deferred to him as 'the professor', and congratulated by Fairbanks, who loved the spoof. Linder was the same age as Fairbanks and things seemed to be looking up after a very difficult period for him during the war, but just two years later, he would be dead in a suicide pact with his young wife at the age of just forty-one.

Dir: Max Linder; **Scr**: Max Linder; **Titles**: Tom Miranda; **Ph**: Harry Vallejo, Max Dupont; **Cast**: Max Linder, Bull Montana, Fred Cavens, Caroline Rankin, Jobyna Ralston.

Tol'able David
US, 1921 – 99 mins
Henry King

Like the lovely rural location of the Virginia mountains, Henry King's pastoral drama *Tol'able David* has plenty of air around it. An opening title on the Museum of Modern Art's print attributes to King the 'gift of repose', by which I think they mean that he has enough confidence in his story structure to take a little time to enjoy the view. There is a hint of nostalgia about the beautiful, remote upland valley, cut off from the world and basking in early summer sunshine.

In the opening scenes, the teenage David Kinemon, the baby of a family of tenant farmers, bounds about the meadow with his dog, bathes in the creek and shows off at 'mumblety-peg' to Esther, the girl next door. The picture created of this idyllic little slice of Americana is completely convincing, from the mother swishing away flies as the family sit down to breakfast, to the village urchins riding illegally on the back of the government mail cart, to David tickling trout in the mountain stream while Esther gazes on admiringly. Henry King grew up in Virginia and that love of home imbues every frame. But this is not time wasted, for it is necessary to establish this idyll for the breaking of it to create the intended depth of emotional response. Moreover, it establishes David's main motivation – to be treated as an adult.

At first, David's attempts at being manly elicit only fond laughter, but then he is forced to grow up quite suddenly, with the arrival in the valley of the Hatburn boys, vicious fugitives who kill his dog and cripple his elder brother. When his father dies, too, weakened by a lifetime's overwork, David has to take on the burden of responsibility for the family but also for the 'Kinemon honor'. His mother refuses to let him take revenge on the Hatburns, and David feels branded as a coward, but of course it is this restraint that is the real rite of passage. As a reviewer in *Photoplay* in February 1921 put it, 'If you can see the scenes with his film mother … without feeling a lump in your throat there's something wrong with you.' The opening scenes also establish the part of David's character that will enable him to grow into the kind of man that he eventually becomes, which is a steely determination to take on a man's work (delivering the government mail), and to defend the family honour and fight his Goliath in the shape of the malicious Luke Hatburn, played with ferocious intensity by Ernest Torrance. The culmination is a no-holds-barred fight to the death (unusually for this period, we see actual blood).

Everything about the film is beautifully crafted – including the scripting by British writer Edmund Goulding and the photography by Henry Cronjager – but it is the direction and the direction of the actors that is most impressive. It is plain to see why Henry King, although few know his name now, was one of the highest-paid directors in Hollywood – only von Stroheim and Lubitsch earned more. For his partner at Inspiration pictures, Richard Barthelmess, it was the part of his life. *Tol'able David* was hailed as a classic instantly on release and age has not tarnished its reputation at all.

Dir: Henry King; **Scr**: Edmund Goulding, Henry King; **Ph**: Henry Cronjager; **Cast**: Richard Barthelmess, Ernest Torrance, Gladys Hulette, Walter P. Lewis, Marion Abbott, Edmund Gurney, Ralph Yearsley.

Topical Budget 93-1 The Derby 1913
UK, 1913 – 4 mins
Topical Film Company

One cannot overstate the importance of newsreels in the development of film – they really deserve a volume of their own. With this in mind, I have chosen just one story that is revealing about newsreels in general but is also an important film in its own right. This is the footage of the 1913 Epsom Derby when the suffragette Emily Davison ran out into the path of the King's horse during the famous race. The cameras of several newsreel companies, including Topical Budget, Pathé Animated Gazette, Gaumont Graphic, Warwick Bioscope Chronicle and Williamson's Animated News, were there to film the event. Fragments of all of these survive, and several managed to capture the actual incident. It was a rare case of the newsreel capturing actual news.

News film, as distinct from newsreel, had existed from the earliest days of moving pictures; in fact, the Derby was one of the first such events ever filmed, by Birt Acres in 1895. It made sense to film the fixtures of the social calendar – they were predictable, topical and had a wide appeal. As the development of purpose-built cinemas increased significantly in 1910/11, guaranteeing regular, reliable audiences, newsreel companies were established to supply news in twice-weekly editions. As well as covering the traditional fixtures – Henley, the Boat Race, the Derby, aviation meetings and so on – and in response to audiences' increasing reliance on the cinemas for news, the rival newsreel cameramen began to film current events such as political meetings, demonstrations, natural disasters and crime. One series of political developments they followed closely were the well-orchestrated demonstrations of the Suffragists. We know that the newsreel companies paid for the rights to film particular events, and the National Union of Women's Suffrage Societies made sure they were filmed. Banners and insignia were designed to be clearly visible in the films, and cameramen were given the best vantage points from which to capture the scale of the demonstrations.

However, one such event where the cameramen would not be expecting to feature a suffragette protest was the Derby, although Emily Davison clearly knew where to stand in order to be caught on film as she ran onto the racecourse. One explanation for this is that the coverage of the Derby was the same, year in year out, building in complexity from Birt Acres's single shot, to the more elaborate films of several minutes' duration. In imitation of the illustrated press and celebrated illustrations of the Derby, like Gustave Doré's *London*, the cameramen covered all the traditions of the Londoner's great day out: the arrival of spectators in perilously overladen vehicles, the poorer citizens travelling by donkey traps, the richer by coach and the intrepid by motor vehicle; the sideshows and betting; the stands and crowds; the start of the race, rounding Tattenham Corner, the finish and beauty shot of the winner. Topical Budget's *The Derby 1913* was no exception, but it also captured the 'accident', in which Davison ran out in front of the King's horse Anmer, was thrown into the air and lay motionless on the ground as a crowd of spectators rushed onto the course to help her and the jockey. Unaware of the gravity of her injuries, the crew carried on shooting and the film was issued that same evening. When Davison died four days later, the images took on a new significance. Watching this film now, it seems callous but at the time, the Topical Budget editors could not have known they had filmed a woman's death. Recycled endlessly for nearly a century, the footage depicts the event in many forms – some with titles that demonstrate awareness of Davison's death, some, like this one, in the version that was issued to cinema audiences on that fateful day.

Prod Co: Topical Film Company.

Underworld
USA, 1927 – 81 mins
Josef von Sternberg

Underworld is mostly known for being a kind of proto-gangster film, a genre that would flourish in the early sound era and go on to develop in all sorts of interesting ways according to the culture of its times – *The Public Enemy* (1931), *Scarface* (1932) and *The Godfather* (1972) being perhaps the most memorable. It is a shame that it is not better known, because it is (I think) one of the most perfect films of the late silent era, made by Josef von Sternberg, one of cinema's greatest auteurs. Part of the problem is that it has been difficult to see until relatively recently and is still slightly compromised by the surviving prints being taken from a 16mm source.

It must have been an incredibly beautiful film in its day (this is obvious even from what remains), and the lighting is exquisite – in particular, the glint shining off Evelyn Brent's black, black eyes. In fact, all of the three protagonists look stunning. Von Sternberg lavishes as much attention on George Bancroft and Clive Brook, with the extensive use of close-ups and long-held shots inviting the viewer's gaze. It is an intimate film, claustrophobically contained within dowdy nightclubs and a safe house. But the outside world is really irrelevant here; this is not a social-issue film, as later gangster films had to be to comply with censorship regulations. In fact, it feels more like a retelling of the Lancelot and Guinevere legend and has a hint of that inescapable tragedy.

'Bull Weed', the gangster king ('Atilla, 2,000 years too late'), as the intertitle tells us, meets a drunk ex-attorney sweeping up in a grimy basement bar, where he is taunted by the lowlifes who throw money into the spittoon to see if he will degrade himself enough to pick it out (a scene Howard Hawks would later borrow for *Rio Bravo* [1959]). Bull sees something in him and gives him a chance to straighten out, which he does to superb effect, becoming a sauve, efficient henchman with beautiful manners, for which Bull dubs him 'Rolls Royce'.

Bull asks him to look after 'Feathers', his moll, and while they are stuck alone in a room together (in a beautifully observed scene), they fall in love, before realising that they both owe Bull their escape from the gutter, creating a bond of loyalty that they can't now betray. The pair struggle to deny themselves, almost driving Rolls Royce back to drink in his despair. There is a wrenchingly painful moment when they fantasise about escape – Bull has been captured and will be hanged, as he was born to; the camera lingers on the suitcase into which the pair put their belongings, then take them out as their resolve to run comes and goes. In the end, conscience compels them to break Bull out of jail.

Thinking they had betrayed him, Bull is reconciled when he discovers they remained loyal and, decisive as ever, he stays behind to take the hail of police bullets while they make their getaway. It is a noble gesture expressed in a little vignette where Bull, under siege in the house and probably about to die, sees that a small kitten has wandered into the chaos. Unconsciously, he picks it up brutally by the scruff and, finding a milk bottle, feeds it from his fingers – it is in his nature to care for those innocents weaker than himself. When he is inevitably recaptured, the police officer asks him what was the point of escaping the noose for so short a time, to which Bull replies, 'That hour was worth more to me than my whole life.'

It is a moving and beautifully written film that earned Ben Hecht the first ever Academy Award for his script.

Dir: Josef von Sternberg; **Scr**: Robert N. Lee, from a story by Ben Hecht; **Ph**: Bert Glennon; **Art Dir**: Hans Dreier; **Cast**: George Bancroft, Evelyn Brent, Clive Brook, Larry Semon.

The Unknown
US, 1927 – 50 mins
Todd Browning

The convention of the Grand Guignol, a small theatre in Paris with a big influence, was for short macabre plays, with sometimes five or six plays making up an evening's entertainment. Horror seems to suit the short form, whether theatrical or literary; it also adapts well to cinema, which is a good medium for delivering the component parts of horror – emotion, shock and atmosphere. Grand Guignol is also essentially naturalistic (sadists not monsters), concerning itself with the more morbid aspects of humanity – death, insanity, mania, sex and horribly ironic coincidence. The sets of the tiny theatre were typically claustrophobic – prison cells, asylums, execution yards, opium dens, brothels, barbershops and operating theatres. Physical deformity of all sorts portrayed through the creative use of make-up was a specialism. Make-up was also the forte of Lon Chaney, star of Tod Browning's gruesome horror *The Unknown*. Written by the director himself, the plot would barely make a short story, but the narrative makes up for it in the neatness of its construction.

The story centres on Alonzo (Lon Chaney), a criminal hiding from the law in a circus as an armless knife-thrower. He has a deformity – two thumbs on his right hand – which is why he pretends to have no arms. He is in love with Nanon (Joan Crawford), who has a phobia (the origins of which are obscure) about men putting their arms around her and therefore feels comfortable only in the presence of Alonzo, who mistakes this genuine affection for love. She is being courted by the strong man Malabar, but flinches every time he tries to touch her. Alonzo strangles Nanon's father, the bullying ringmaster, when he discovers Alonzo's secret. The murder is witnessed by the horrified Nanon, who sees his two thumbs but not his face. Determined to have Nanon and unable now to tell her the truth, Alonzo is driven to the drastic step of blackmailing a surgeon to amputate his arms. The glimpse of the operating theatre is one of the grislier moments in the film. He stays away to convalesce long enough for Nanon to overcome her phobia under the patient ministrations of Malabar. Having made this terrible sacrifice, only to find himself rejected, tips him into insanity and he plots a fitting end for Malabar (yes, it does involve arms) that spectacularly backfires in a moment of supreme poetic justice.

Many of the Guignol tropes are in evidence – the lowlife setting of the carnival, the depravity of the anti-hero, the psycho-sexual phobia of the heroine that borders on titillation, the oppositional pairing of the strong man with the armless Alonzo and the appropriateness of the revenge. But it is only Lon Chaney who could pull off this improbable story. Joan Crawford famously said that it was watching him at work on *The Unknown* that taught her the difference between acting and standing around in front of the camera. Chaney was not only able to put up with the extreme discomfort that must have been necessary for the role, but he could convey profound emotion – it is relatively rare to see tears at this period, so one is taken aback by the almost unbearable pathos. His performance elevates the film from kitsch to classic.

Dir: Todd Browning; **Scr**: Waldemar Young; **Ph**: Merritt B. Gerstad; **Cast**: Lon Chaney, Joan Crawford, Nick de Ruiz, Norman Kerry, John George.

Les Vampires
France, 1915 – 440 mins
Louis Feuillade

Populist and pulpy, there are few silent films as accessible to us today as the great serials of Louis Feuillade. Between 1913 and 1922, the film serial, surfing a great wave of public fascination initiated by the Fantômas crime stories, was a vibrant, inventive and addictive genre, which the box-set junkies of today will tune into easily. These French serials have only been made widely accessible quite recently – most of the American examples are still not available – so modern audiences have rarely had a chance to get hooked on them. They are a problem to programme, racking up 7 or 8 hours of running time, and so won't fit conveniently into the cinema exhibition structure based on the 90-minute feature. The only really satisfactory way to see them is an episode or two a day at a week-long festival – frequent enough not to forget the story but not in back-to-back episodes so that plot repetitions become tedious. With the advent of DVD and internet streaming sites, you can (sort of) replicate this experience for yourself, although you miss out on the glorious quality of the photography.

It is its modern appeal that made me choose *Les Vampires* of all the serials. It isn't the best, or necessarily the most compelling, but the themes and aesthetics seem to have had a greater influence down the years, not only in the obvious references such as Olivier Assayas's postmodern feature *Irma Vep* (1996) but in the aesthetic of *Modesty Blaise* or *The Avengers*, as well as a host of Italian series of the 1960s, such as *Diabolik*. It's the 'look' that creates the sense of familiarity for the modern audience. Many film directors and artists (Chabrol, Resnais, the Surrealists, Buñuel) were influenced by the look of *Les Vampires*, with its realist setting, ultra-modern automobiles, amoral tone and skin-tight black catsuits. The film was issued intermittently in ten parts, each comprising four or five episodes with sensational titles such as 'The Severed Head' and 'The Bloody Wedding'. The principal protagonist is a

Irma Vep spreads her wings in Feuillade's sensational serial

journalist, Phillipe Guérande, who, with his bumbling sidekick Mazamette, is pursuing a gang of criminals known as 'Les Vampires' who have infiltrated every aspect of society in Paris and beyond. They steal jewels from the rich by impersonating members of high society or by cat thievery, lone figures clambering over the rooftops at night, appearing and disappearing though trapdoors and false fireplaces.

The high priestess of this band is Irma Vep, played by stage star Musidora, who is a master of disguise, appearing as a society lady or a boy or in her trademark vampiric black suit. She is seen variously as the mistress of the grand vampire or as the lover of the charismatic Moreno, head of a rival gang, signalling her amorality but also her independence. The concerns of the gang have often been associated with anarchist bands of the day, such as the illegalist Bonnot Gang, the first to use an automobile as a getaway from a bank robbery; such gangs may have had an influence on Feuillade, given his penchant for robbery, suburban Paris streets and automobiles, but in fact, apart from the slight hint of free love, the gang members are straightforward but very well-organised thieves. Scandalous enough in 1915, Irma Vep's strong, criminal female lead is only one of many attractions, including the constantly moving (and occasionally clever) plot, the beautiful locations and settings, high production values full of real trains, big explosions, good stunts and, not least, the dynamic tinting – there is a moment when Moreno turns a light on and off several times to signal to his gang outside which is indicated by switching from amber to purple and back again.

Les Vampires, with *Fantômas* (1913), spawned a decade of superior serial production in France, including *Judex* (1916), *Tih Minh* (1918), *Barrabas* (1919) and *La Maison du mystère* (1921), all hugely enjoyable and which we can only hope will become more widely available one day.

Dir/Scr: Louis Feuillade; **Ph**: Manichoux; **Cast**: Musidora, Edouard Mathé, Marcel Lévesque, Jean Aymé, Louis Leubas, Bout-de-Zan.

Voyage à travers l'impossible (*The Impossible Voyage*)
France, 1904 – 20 mins
Georges Méliès

Georges Méliès's major love was the popular theatre of the late nineteenth century. He sold his interest in the family firm to buy the Théâtre Robert-Houdin in 1888, an establishment specialising in magic shows. He had spent time at a similar venue in London, Maskelyne's Egyptian Theatre, and imported many of its acts (David Devant's 'Vanishing Lady', for example), forming connections that would prove useful when the arrival of moving pictures gave them all the opportunity to combine this new novelty into their respective set-ups. Like Devant, he bought his first projector from R. W. Paul and began to show Paul and Edison films in Paris. With the aid of the technical staff he inherited as part of the assets of the theatre, he built his own camera and, using existing sets and costumes and a plethora of ingenious stage devices, went into production for himself. Like other pioneer producers, he produced simple actualities and reconstructions of topical world events, but it was his love of theatrical spectacle that he wanted to bring to his audiences.

He soon built a glass studio with a fully working stage based on exactly the same dimensions as his theatre, so presumably he could use existing equipment. His profound knowledge of the mechanics of illusions, the smooth continuity facilitated by the well-planned entrances and exits, ramps and traps required to move the actors, dioramas with which to simulate movement in the backgrounds and flyaway scenery to suggest depth, coupled with a flair for photographic trickery and lighting effects, enabled Méliès to produce prestige films of the magic tricks and fantasy spectacles that could be found in his beloved Parisian theatres.

The delightful *A Trip to the Moon* (1902), based on a Jules Verne novel, is nowadays his best-known film, but take a look at *Voyage à travers l'impossible*, made at the height of his career, for the full range of stage and film tricks, beautiful colouring, fantastical devices, dancing girls,

Master magician Georges Méliès conjures up planes, trains and automobiles

comedians, even Méliès himself as Professor Mabouloff. The story, like *Trip to the Moon*, is based on a fantasy journey taken by means of a variety of crazy vehicles – a train, a car, a dirigible, a submarine and, oddly, a refrigerated van. There is an expository prologue at the Institute of Incoherent Geography, in which the plans for a voyage round the world are put to the committee. We see the preparations for the voyage in the machine shop (beautifully rendered with perspective painting and moving scenery) before the party of explorers sets off in the train. They experience various adventures: the train flies across the sky, they go to the surface of the sun, past the stars and planets, which are alternately painted and personified, and after a series of crashes and rescues by their crazy vehicle, they drop back to Earth, landing in the sea and finally exploding back onto terra firma and the congratulatory epilogue.

At 20 minutes long, this was a very expensive production taking months to set up and cost a staggering 37,000 francs, but the attention to detail, popular subject matter (based again on a Jules Verne story and

Adolphe Dennery's spectacular play) and high production values made it a success and it sold ninety-five copies in its first week in the US alone. Méliès was the master of these exuberant and very personal productions. Essentially an individual producer/performer of illusions, despite a level of success, he could never have operated on the industrial scale of the major companies like Pathé and Gaumont, or wanted to. His films are a fascinating record of the bygone era of the nineteenth-century theatre and are as entertaining as ever.

Dir: Georges Méliès.

Way Down East
US, 1920 – 120 mins
D. W. Griffith

A criticism often levelled at D. W. Griffith's later features is that they were increasingly out of touch – old-fashioned Victorian melodramas that held no appeal for the modern audience – and that was the reason for his fall from grace as cinema's most important director. This lazy theory ignores the fact that adaptations of Victorian drama were big business before, during and after his version of *Way Down East* was released in 1920 (and their popularity shows no signs of abating to date). The audiences for it were huge and it was a major success, being reissued several times. The play, by no means the hokey old melodrama of received wisdom, had a twenty-year track record before the film version appeared and continued to tour profitably long after the film's release. Griffith allegedly paid $175,000 for this property, which tells its own story. If he failed to establish himself as a major producer during these years, it was certainly not the fault of his choice of source material for this film, which many regard as his masterwork.

Way Down East works better than any of his previous features in terms of the cohesion and intimacy of the story, focusing on one main character and following her traumatic story to a satisfying resolution. It relies heavily on the acting skills of Lillian Gish but the details, so thoroughly road-tested in the stage play and a subsequent novel, support the performance and plot. This is simple enough. Anna, played by Gish, is a poor New England village girl, who, on a visit to rich relatives in the city, is seduced by a wealthy womaniser, Lennox Sanderson. He stages a mock wedding to get her into bed, then abandons her when she falls pregnant. Motherless, broke and pregnant, Anna finds herself in a dingy boarding house where the baby dies in a scene as harrowing as only Lillian Gish could make it. Cast out for being unmarried, she walks the

(*Opposite page*) Lillian Gish in deadly peril as the ice floes break up

country roads until she happens on the Bartlett's farm, a thriving, happy place exhibiting Christian charity and tolerance. In this Arcadia, she meets and falls in love with David, the son of the house, but because of her past she feels unfit to marry him when he asks. Eventually, in a duo of Hardyesque coincidences, Anna's past catches up with her and she is cast out once more into a blizzard to face almost certain death when she faints from cold on the ice floes as the river flows inexorably over a weir.

The drama is good and perfectly paced – it is a film with no dead spots – but it is the structural and textural details that make the film. There are a lot of contrasts – town and country, the theme of poetry and courtly love versus reality. In one instance of the latter, the seducer chooses to compare Anna's beauty to that of Elaine the lily maid (the source for the Lady of Shallot, an apt image of one who was famously dumped by Launcelot and after killing herself, floated down the river in a boat to Camelot). This piece of pretension is represented by a fantasy scene in which Anna is shown in medieval garb against an obviously cardboard setting, showing up the fantasy for the sham it is. David and Anna's courtship, on the other hand, takes place on a real riverbank. Early in the plot, we have seen them as psychically connected. David wakes from a nightmare when Anna is abandoned and desperate, sensing her before her arrival at the farm; a bird, which perhaps symbolises the poetic nature of his soul, later nestles in Anna's hand as she thinks of him. All this builds to the final famous scene on the ice floes as Nature, as ever, tops the human crisis and puts their petty problems into their proper perspective.

Dir: D. W. Griffith; **Scr**: Anthony Paul Kelly, from *Way Down East* by William A. Brady, based on the play by Lottie Blair Parker; **Ph**: Billy Bitzer; **Cast**: Lillian Gish, Richard Barthelmess, Lowell Sherman, Vivia Ogden.

The White Slave Trade (*Den hvide slavehandel*)
Denmark, 1910 – 32 mins
August Blom

The years 1910 and 1911 were pivotal to the development of the cinema, marking the huge expansion of purpose-built cinemas, the birth of the feature film, the consolidation of the industry, the rise of the distributor over the exhibitor and the establishment of the newsreel. As ever in moments of change in the film industry, key film titles were involved. Of all the productions that caught the popular imagination, the interest of the press and the financial interests of the distributors, none was more significant than the Danish film *The White Slave Trade*. It helped to spark off the golden age of Danish cinema and heralded an era in which it became worthwhile for exhibitors to build bigger, more lavish cinemas, and for film companies to organise and attract investment – all underpinned by the public's desire for longer films. The model of the mixed programme changed to accommodate the longer multi-reel film that allowed for character and story development and for the exposition that would enable film-makers to adapt culturally prestigious works more effectively for the screen. It also spawned huge numbers of sensational films on the subject of white slavery.

But how was it that the public came to express this preference, how did it come to their attention? The key factor was probably sensationalist marketing (see also *L'Inferno**), but it is important first to establish that the title applies to two different productions – the earlier and slightly longer film directed by Alfred Cohn for Fotorama and released in February 1910, and the later copy directed by August Blom for Nordisk in August of that year. Only the latter survives, which is my reason for choosing it over the other. Shamelessly pirating the original, shot for shot, it used the same name as the successful Fotorama film. To dodge charges of plagiarism it was distributed in different territories, mainly abroad. It was an instant hit, no doubt due to its topical and lurid nature. It built on a social panic across Europe and America and it is no coincidence that the story is located in London (indicated neatly, if cheaply, by showing Big Ben out of a window), that vast metropolis and den of vice, heaving with foreign villains but also home to wily detectives and the strong arm of Scotland Yard. The story is replete with deceptions – the innocent heroine Anna is lured to London by a false letter. There is an elegant conflation – a split-screen triptych, with two of the villains speaking on the telephone across a shot of Anna and her father on their way to the harbour, innocently walking into the white slavers' trap. On arrival, she is captured and confined in a brothel, where she is locked up and beaten to break her spirit, and then sold to a debauched aristocrat; but a sympathetic maid helps her and contacts the detective, Fabian. A series of escapes and chases ensue. The police catch up with the villains in a thrilling rooftop climax.

It is easy to draw a direct line from this film to the sensational serials that were to come in the next few years and to the huge numbers of white slave trade films that succeeded it. Blom's own sequel, *Hvide slavehandel sidste offer* (1911), considerably heightened the violence (and, consequently, the suspense or titillation) of the beating scenes in the brothel, which were in turn heightened in *Traffic in Souls* (1913). A sub-series of films, in which Mormons replaced 'foreigners' as the kidnappers, continued to appeal even into the 1920s with films like *Trapped by the Mormons* (1922).

Dir: August Blom; **Ph**: Axel Sørensen; **Cast**: Ellen Diedrich, Lauritz Olsen, Ella La Cour, Victor Fabian, Svend Bille, Einar Zangenberg.

The Wind
US, 1928 – 78 mins
Victor Sjöström

A delicately reared young girl (Letty) has travelled from the east to the
Texan plain, a hostile dry place of incessant, maddening winds.
Ejected from her only relative's ranch by a jealous wife, she is standing in
a dirty, wooden shack married to a comparative stranger (Lige), who is
trying to kiss her. She recoils. He tries to put her at ease by bringing
coffee, she can't drink it, and tips it into the water jug when he's not
looking; but later, he finds out and, having tried everything he can think
of to please her, storms out slamming the tin coffee cup on the floor.
On their wedding night, they pace one each side of a locked door,
unable to break the deadlock. Resigned, he picks up the flimsy cup and
carefully begins to press out the dents he has made during his passionate
outburst. This is the critical scene in *The Wind*, a beautifully observed and
constructed tour de force of the late silent cinema.

 Its director, Victor Sjöström, famously had a natural empathy with
landscape and the forces of nature, and also, I would argue, for the
woman's point of view. This made him a good choice to direct this very
female-focused project, an adaptation of Dorothy Scarborough's
remarkable Texan novel, which Lillian Gish had suggested to Irving
Thalberg at MGM as a follow-up from their success with *The Scarlet
Letter* (1926). Another woman, Frances Marion, wrote the scenario.
It helps to look at *The Wind* from a female perspective in order to
understand the sexual symbolism, which runs all through the picture.
The wind, which is repeated as visual metaphor throughout, represents
male lust, the perils of the natural world and animal passions – in its
more extreme manifestation, it is shown as a white stallion raging in the
gale. Letty is as terrified of the wind as she is of sex, and it begins to
unhinge her. When Roddy, a former flirtation, reappears with the
intention of seducing her, visualisations of the wind are equated with the
threat of his lust. Lige is obliged to leave her to round up the wild horses,

allowing Roddy to get her alone as the storm rises. The shack is shaking itself to bits and the wind batters at the door. Almost driven demented by it, she suddenly realises that the knocking at the door is a person – we see a fist hammering at it from the other side. She lets him in, the door bursting open with the force of the storm, then realising it is not Lige, tries to escape but is literally blown by the wind back against him. The symbolism here is very plain.

The ending has often been seen as problematic, as Gish later stated that the studio forced them to tack on a happy ending, but it seems to me remarkably successful. Letty's fear of sex is overcome, albeit in a most brutal way, and in the final shot, when released from fear by her reconciliation with Lige, she adopts a liberated, erotically charged pose (not unlike the white stallion with its mane blowing in the wind), which seems to mesh perfectly with the preceding imagery. The wind has blown someone some good after all. No evidence has ever come to light of a tragic ending in Frances Marion's draft scripts, and that pose must have been a very deliberate choice by Gish, so that it is open to speculation whether the actress was trying to justify the film's lack of box-office success by the usual means of blaming the management. She needn't have worried, with Sjöström's microcosmic attention to detail and her ardent performance, *The Wind* is rightly seen as a classic.

Dir: Victor Sjöström (as Victor Seastrom); **Ph**: John Arnold; **Scr**: Frances Marion; **Cast**: Lillian Gish, Lars Hanson, Montagu Love, Dorothy Cumming, William Orlamond.

Witchcraft through the Ages (**Häxan**)
Sweden/Denmark, 1922 – 82 mins
Benjamin Christensen

One might be forgiven for thinking that all Danish and Swedish
film-makers are fixated on medieval obsessions with demonology and
death – Sjöström's *The Phantom Carriage**, Dreyer's *Day of Wrath* (1943),
Bergman's *The Seventh Seal* (1956), for example. Arguably, this started
with Benjamin Christensen's *Häxan*, made between 1919 and 1921,
a film which has piqued the interest of successive generations.
The enduring appeal, of course, is horror – the film has plenty of magic,
demonology, grotesquery, religious hypocrisy, torture and a surprising
level of untamed eroticism. What seems to confuse some film historians
and theorists, if not the general public, is the film's format. Is it a
documentary, a drama-doc, an illustrated lecture?

   Christensen, already a celebrated director after his storming debut
with *The Mysterious X* (1913), spent two years filming this history of the
medieval worldview, the inquisitions against witchcraft, our
contemporary treatment of the old and poor, and, post-Freud, the
treatment of psychiatric problems. Given his curiosity about the subject
and assuming that it was not merely lascivious, it is interesting to
speculate how he could have made the film within the conventional
forms of the day – would he have got away with a straight narrative
fiction feature? Absolutely not. But as a scholarly treatise, it had more
chance. A *Variety* reviewer summed it up perfectly, 'Wonderful though
this picture is, it is absolutely unfit for public exhibition.'[29] What could be
more inviting?

   Following this opening exposition, the film presents a series of
vignettes showing, in very graphic detail, the witches' lair with full
complement of gruesomeness – a thief's hand cut from the gallows,
flying ointment, love potions, wretched and deformed crones, etc.
This proceeds to an accusation of witchcraft and the persecution of an
old woman, who, under torture, confesses to flying on broomsticks; and

A witches' sabbath in this unusual dramatised documentary

there are midnight sabbaths in which religious icons are abused, dead babies boiled, witches kiss Satan's behind and consort with randy demons. The concluding chapter, which examines contemporary attitudes to the strange behaviour of women (labelled here as hysteria), is the one part of the film that dates.

Aside from this, the most notable thing about *Häxan*, apart from the shock of the nudity and sexual content, and the creepiness of the demons, with their excellent costumes and make-up, is its film-making quality. Christensen gives full credit to his cameraman Johan Ankerstjerne and art director Richard Louw, who, over the two years of its production, came up with a succession of fabulous and beautifully executed special effects. The multi-layered shot of the witches' midnight ride, in particular, exemplifies that quality. The eerily lit witches ride across the sky (with lateral and vertical movement), superimposed on a travelling shot over the roofs of the town (a convincing model shot that also revolves), followed by a misty sky background (also moving laterally) and a silhouette matte of the hilltop at night with the outline of a naked witch and an owl on a blasted oak. Woodland sets are also used to obscure our view of the devilries of the witches' sabbath, making us want to see more. The film is a catalogue of effects and techniques, including stop-motion animation, superimposition, silhouette and matte work, and expressive lighting, that are way in advance of later horror films. Added to this is the editing, which makes the most of the short take to allow tantalising glimpses of horrors unknown and unspeakable sexual perversions. It is that quality as well as the theme that makes *Häxan* timeless.

Dir/Scr: Benjamin Christensen; **Ph**: Johan Ankerstjerne; **Art Dir**: Richard Louw; **Cast**: Benjamin Christensen, Astrid Holm, Ella la Cour, Maren Pedersen, Johannes Andersen, Tora Teje.

Notes

1. Judi Freeman, 'Bridging Purism and Surrealism: The Origins and Production of Fernand Léger's Ballet Mécanique', in Rudolf E. Kuenzli (ed.), *Dada and Surrealist Film* (London and Cambridge, MA: MIT Press, 1996), p. 31.

2. Ibid.

3. Ibid., p. 29.

4. Geoffrey Malins, *How I Filmed the War* (London: Herbert Jenkins, 1922), p. 162.

5. C. A. Lejeune, *Manchester Guardian*, 16 September 1927.

6. Quoted in Richard Taylor, *The Battleship Potemkin: The Film Companion* (London and New York: Tauris, 2000), p. 95.

7. Margaret Kennedy, *The Mechanised Muse* (London: George Allen & Unwin/P.E.N. Books, 1942).

8. Charles Musser, 'To Redream the Dream of White Playwrights: Reappropriation and Resistance in Oscar Micheaux's Body and Soul', in Pearl Bowser, Jane Gaines and Charles Musser (eds), *Oscar Micheaux and His Circle: African American Film-making and Race Cinema in the Silent Era* (Bloomington: Indiana University Press, 2001).

9. Edgar Allan Poe, 'The Philosophy of Composition', *Graham's Magazine*, April 1846.

10. Donald McCaffrey, *Focus on Chaplin* (Englewood Cliffs, NJ: Prentice-Hall, 1971), p. 85.

11. Carlos Flores, *Les lliçons de Gaudí* (Barcelona: Editorial Empúries, 2002), p. 89. See <http://en.wikipedia.org/wiki/Antoni_Gaud%C3%AD>.

12. Robert E. Sherwood, *Life*, 1 January 1925, p. 24.

13. Richard Kozarski, *An Evening's Entertainment: The Age of the Silent Feature Picture 1915–1928* (New York: Scribners, 1990), p. 9.

14. Guy Maddin, interviewed by Michael Brooke, *Vertigo*, vol. 2 no. 6 (Spring 2004), p. 24. Available online at: <http://www.vertigomagazine.co.uk/showarticle.php?sel=bac&siz=1&id=435>.

15. *Bioscope* supplement, 19 December 1912.

16. Dziga Vertov, quoted in Yuri Tsivian, *Lines of Resistance: Dziga Vertov and the Twenties* (Pordenone: Le Giornate del Cinema Muto, 2004).

17. Richard W. Bann, 'Leo McCarey at Hal Roach Studios'. Available online at: <www.laurelundhardy.de/archive/articles/1998-10-mccarey-long.html>.

18. Yuri Tsivian, film commentary, *Man with a Movie Camera* DVD (BFI, 2008).

19. Walt Whitman, 'City of Ships', 'Mannahatta', 'Crossing Brooklyn Ferry', 'A Broadway Pageant', 'Song of the Broad-Axe' (from the collection *Leaves of Grass*, 1855).

20. Robert J. Flaherty, 'How I Filmed Nanook of the North: Adventures with the Eskimos to Get Pictures of Their Home Life and Their Battles with Nature to Get Food. The Walrus Fight', *World's Work*, October 1922, p. 632.

21. Kevin Brownlow, *Napoleon: Abel Gance's Classic Film* (London: BFI Publishing, 2004).

22. Interestingly, Henri Chrétien, who invented CinemaScope, attended the Opéra premiere of *Napoléon* in Paris in 1927. His invention had originally been intended for military use (as a 180-degree viewer for tanks).

23. Christopher Frayling, film commentary, *Nosferatu* DVD (BFI, 2002).

24. See, for example, *Day of the Triffids* (1962), *Omega Man* (1971), *28 Days Later* (2002), *I Am Legend* (2007), and many more.

25. 'Crossing the line' or the 180-degree rule is a reverse-angle cut in which the relationship between two figures is shown in mirror image, creating a disorienting effect.

26. Kurt Siodmak, interviewed by Dennis Fischer, in Pat McGilligan (ed.), *Interviews with Screenwriters of the 1940s and 1950s* (Berkeley and Los Angeles: University of California Press, 1991). See <http://notesoncinematograph.blogspot.com/2010/08/im-poor-writer-curt-siodmak-on-siodmaks.html>.

27. Joris Ivens, *The Camera and I* (New York: International Publishers, 1969), p. 36.

28. Lynda Nead, *The Haunted Gallery: Painting, Photography, Film c. 1900* (New Haven, CT, and London: Yale University Press, 2007).

29. *Variety*, 31 March 1922.

Bibliography

Abel, Richard, *French Cinema: The First Wave 1915–1929* (Princeton, NJ: Princeton University Press, 1992).

——, *The Ciné Goes to Town: French Cinema 1896–1914* (Bloomington, IN: University of California Press, 2nd edn., 1998).

Blum, Daniel, *A Pictorial History of the Silent Screen* (London: Spring Books, 1966).

Brownlow, Kevin, *The Parade's Gone By* (London: Secker & Warburg, 1968).

——, *The War, the West and the Wilderness* (London: Secker & Warburg, 1979).

——, *Napoleon* (London: Photoplay Productions, 2004).

Cherchi Usai, Paolo, *Silent Cinema: An Introduction* (London: BFI, 2000).

Low, Rachael, *History of the British Film*, vols. 1–4, 1896–1929 (London: George Allen & Unwin, 1973).

Mayer, David, *Stagestruck Filmmaker: D. W. Griffith and the American Theatre* (Iowa City: University of Iowa Press, 2009).

Nowell-Smith, Geoffrey (ed.), *The Oxford History of World Cinema* (Oxford: Oxford University Press, 1996).

O'Leary, Liam, *The Silent Cinema* (London: Studio Vista/Dutton, 1965).

Salt, Barry, *Film Style and Technology: History and Analysis* (London: Starword, 2003).

Thompson, Kristin, and David Bordwell, *Film History: An Introduction* (New York: McGraw-Hill, 1994).

Online sources

More and more information is being put online so that it is relatively easy now to get basic information on all films. The following sites are particularly useful:

IMDB:

BFI Film and Television Database: <www.bfi.org.uk/filmtvinfo/ftvdb/>

BFI screenonline:

Also, try the website and databases of members of FIAF (International

Federation of Film Archives):
<www.fiafnet.org/uk/>
There are numerous very good specialist
silent cinema and general cinema
blogs, along with the specialist film
festival websites. For a comprehensive
guide to all aspects of silent film, go to
.

Index

Page numbers in **bold** (used for titles, directors and in a few iconic cases stars) indicate a film's main entry; those in *italic* denote illustrations.

List of Illustrations

While considerable effort has been made to correctly identify the copyright holders this has not been possible in all cases. We apologise for any apparent negligence and any omissions or corrections brought to our attention will be remedied in any future editions.

Alice in Wonderland, Hepworth & Co.; *Ballet mécanique*, Fernand Léger–Dudley Murphy; *The Battleship Potemkin*, First Studio Goskino; *Beggars of Life*, © Paramount Famous Lasky Corporation; *The Big Swallow*, Williamson Kinematograph Company; *Blackmail*, British International Pictures; *The Cabinet of Dr. Caligari*, Decla Filmgesellschaft; *Casanova*, Universal Films de France/Cinémathèque Française; *Un Chien andalou*, Salvador Dalí/Louis Buñuel; *Earth*, Ukrainfilm; *Finis terrae*, Société Genérale de Films; *The General*, © Joseph M. Schenck; *The Golem, How He Came into the World*, Ufa; *Gösta Berlings Saga*, Svensk Filmindustri; *How a Mosquito Operates*, Vitagraph Company of America; *It*, © Famous Players–Lasky Corporation; *I Was Born, But …*, © Shochiku Co. Ltd; *The Informer*, British International Pictures; *The Kid*, © Charles Chaplin Corporation; *The Lure of Crooning Water*, Stoll Film Company; *Napoléon*, Films Historiques/Westi/Société Générale de Films; *The Nibelungen Saga*, Decla Gesellschaft for Ufa; *Nosferatu: A Symphony of Horrors*, Prana-Film; *Pandora's Box*, Nero-Film; *Paris qui dort*, Films Diamant; *The Phantom Carriage*, Svensk Filmindustri; *Safety Last!*, Pathé Exchange/Hal Roach Studios; *La Souriante Madame Beudet*, Vandal-Delac-Aubert; *The Son of the Sheik*, Feature Productions; *Stage Struck*, © Famous Players–Lasky Corporation; *Suspense*, Rex Motion Picture Company; *Les Vampires*, Film Gaumont; *Voyage à travers l'impossible*, Star-Film; *Way Down East*, D. W. Griffith; *Witchcraft through the Ages*, Svensk Filmindustri.